Babe Ruth's Ghost

Babe Ruth's Ghost

AND OTHER HISTORICAL
AND LITERARY SPECULATIONS

Louis D. Rubin, Jr.

UNIVERSITY OF WASHINGTON PRESS
SEATTLE AND LONDON

Copyright @ 1996 by the University of Washington Press
Printed in the United States of America
All rights reserved. No portion of this publication may be reproduced
or transmitted in any form or by any means, electronic or mechanical,
including photocopy, recording, or any information storage or retrieval
system without permission in writing from the publisher.

Library of Congress Cataloging-in-Publication Data

Rubin, Louis Decimus, 1923–
    Babe Ruth's ghost and other historical and literary speculations /
Louis D. Rubin, Jr.
        p.   cm.
    ISBN 0-295-97529-6 (cloth : alk. paper).—ISBN 0-295-97530-x
(pbk. : alk. paper)
    1. American literature—History and criticism. 2. History, Modern—
20th century. I. Title
PS121.R77 1996
814'.54—dc20   95-52732
                                                                    CIP

The text paper used in this publication is acid-free and recycled from
10% post-consumer and at least 50% pre-consumer waste. The text and
insert papers meet the minimum requirements of American National Standard for Information Sciences—Permanence of Paper for Printed Library
Materials, ANSI Z39.48-1984

For the Hollins crowd
in & around Chapel Hill:
Lee, Cindy, Mimi, Shannon, Wyndham
as being the very best

Contents

Of All the World's Great Heroes

Did Churchill 'Ruin The Great Work of Time'? Thoughts on the New British Revisionism

> *[Who] Could by industrious valor climb*
> *To ruin the great work of Time,*
> *And cast the kingdom old*
> *Into another mold. . . .*
> —Marvell, *Horatian Ode Upon Cromwell's*
> *Return from Ireland*

Writers of history have always been good at second guessing; in large measure it is their trade. These days the history of the Second World War is currently being rewritten by certain young British historians, who are eager to show that it was all a dreadful mistake, and the British should have stayed out and allowed the Germans and Russians to fight each other until exhausted, thereby preserving the Empire and keeping the Americans from taking over.

In such a thesis, the heroes are the sometime appeasers—Neville Chamberlain, Stanley Baldwin, Neville Henderson, Viscount Halifax, Sir Samuel Hoare, Sir John Simon, and the others who sought to placate Adolf Hitler and keep the Germans turned eastward in search of new countries to conquer. The villain, naturally enough, is Winston Churchill, whose great speech of defiance—"we shall fight on the landing grounds, we shall fight in the fields and in the streets, we shall fight in the hills, we shall never surrender. . . . "—was no

3

more than "sublime nonsense." The verdict is John Charmley's, in *Churchill: The End of Glory,* the American edition of which was published late in 1993 by Harcourt Brace Jovanovich.

It was nonsense, the argument goes, because in June 1940, with French resistance crumbling and the victorious *Wehrmacht* setting up operations along the English Channel coast, the only way that Hitler could be stopped was by getting the United States involved. To do that, it would be necessary to mortgage all one's imperial wealth and possessions to the Americans, who would surely take advantage of the situation to become the dominant power, happily drain Britain of her resources, and leave her bereft of empire, prosperity, and *amour-propre.* To quote Charmley again, "It was certainly better to be an American rather than a German protectorate, but given that the war was being fought to preserve Britain's independence and a balance of power, that reflection was of little comfort to many Englishmen."

Neville Chamberlain and the Conservative leadership realized that Britain couldn't afford to wage another world war, and that even if the war were won she would wind up in hock to the Yanks—who in Mr. Charmley's words "were, in fact, foreigners who disliked the British Empire even more than did Hitler." So the Tory leadership did their best to conciliate the *Führer,* and when that failed and they were obliged to declare war, they planned to sit tight and do nothing that might cause trouble. But that didn't work, either, so when Hitler invaded and overran France and the Low Countries, they were prepared to face up to the facts of life and seek to arrange a peace agreement.

Alas, Winston Churchill wouldn't let them get away with it. Filled with romantic dreams of glory and sentimental nostalgia for the nineteenth century, the far-flung battle line, and dominion over palm and pine, he insisted that Britain was in the war to defeat Nazi Germany, and there was no alternative to military victory. Not only did he think it would be "certainly better to be an American rather than a German protectorate," but he was sufficiently deluded to believe that acquiescence in a Nazi-dominated Europe would be unthinkable, that no treaty with Hitler would be worth the paper it was printed on for very long, and that an England that might be permitted to carry on under Adolf Hitler's sufferance would be no England worth living in at all.

So, instead of seeking an agreement that would have enabled Britain to hold onto its cash reserves and keep its Empire intact, Churchill insisted on the expenditure of "blood, toil, tears and sweat" in order to "wage war, by sea, land and air, with all our might and with all the strength that God can give us" in pursuit of "Victory—victory at all costs."

Thus misled, the British people stood up to Hitler long enough for the United States and the Soviet Union to join the fray, with the result that Nazi Germany was defeated. The price of national honor turned out to be financial bankruptcy, loss of the Empire, the end of British status as a world power, Soviet domination of eastern Europe, and American leadership of the Free World—in short, the End of Glory.

So argues John Charmley, in a revisionist biography whose 649 pages of text and 52 pages of double-columned notes belie the fact that it is in inception and execution a partisan tract, with an animus against its subject that will grant him absolutely nothing. The Winston Churchill of this volume is an almost unmitigated disaster to his country. To find this book's counterpart one must turn to the debunking biographies of the 1920s, or Lytton Strachey on Cardinal Manning, or John T. Flynn on F. D. R., or perhaps H. L. Mencken on Woodrow Wilson.

That Sir Winston was a flawed human, who made mistakes, that he was no stranger either to ambition or to egocentricity, has long been known. But that he recognized the evil of Nazi Germany almost at once when others did not, and led his island nation in a heroic fight to preserve its freedom, and in so doing—and in no merely metaphorical sense—saved the Western world, has been generally conceded.

What is happening now, however, is that as memories of those days and the emotions they evoked have ebbed, a new school of historians has come forth, whose members never knew the sound of air-raid sirens or the drone of buzz bombs, heard the *Führer*'s voice over the wireless pledging vengeance upon England, or sang "There'll Always Be an England." What's so great about having saved the Western world from the Nazis? they want to know. Why wasn't Adolf Hitler allowed to go his own way unhindered, and the people of Continental Europe left to fend for themselves? What did the deaths of millions of European Jews, Slavs, and others matter in the scheme of things?

II

Revisionist history-writing is, of course, no new phenomenon. These days it is characteristic of the British right; in the 1960s and 1970s the revisionists were from the political left. What is common to all such activity is the intent to effect a violent reversal of the reigning historical consensus, whatever that may happen to be at the time. The young historians of the New Left in the 1960s and 1970s were busily proving that the Cold War was a conspiracy of American imperialism, and the Marshall Plan no more than a scheme for the economic victimization of the Third World. The motive for all this was obvious: it was a way of protesting against the war in Vietnam. What better way to do that, if one were a historian, than to demonstrate that one's elders were self-serving hypocrites, who used pious platitudes to cloak cynical aggressiveness and economic buccaneering?

To say this is not to contend that there is no place for revised interpretation of the past, or that the reasons why people say and believe that they have acted at various junctures in history are necessarily sacred. Unexamined assumptions, half-truths, fallible judgments, and special pleadings have ever been the way of humankind. At the same time, though, if there is one thing that may be learned from the study of historiography, it is that the needs and the values of the historian's own time play an important part in the interpretation of the past. Nor need one be an historical relativist to acknowledge the difficulties of any attempt to put oneself in the place of the historical figures of a different era, and to see the world and their place within it as they viewed such things. Human nature itself may not change very much, but the terms whereby that nature expresses itself can differ profoundly from one era to another.

The revisionist impulse, however, involves more than merely an impulse to interpret the past anew. There is, after all, a considerable difference between recognizing that the assumptions of an historian's own day are bound to color any assessment of the past, and setting out to write history with the fervent conviction that all previous efforts to interpret the subject one is scrutinizing were no more than willful distortions of truth, compounded of mythology and self-congratulation, and therefore crying out for unmasking.

What propels the dedicated revisionist is the urgent desire to upset the applecart, and to play the role of fearless exposer of the previous generation's historical evasions, clever distortions, and crafty cover-ups. Add to this a *soupçon* of *épater le bourgeois*, and you have not only John Charmley and today's young Brits, but the writing of history as a species of parricide.

III

The current World War II revisionism is emanating principally from political conservatives—Charmley describes himself as a right-wing Thatcherite. No breathtaking imaginative leap is needed to recognize why this might be so. Great Britain is not only no longer a major political and military power, but in industrial and economic position it has receded to the second rank. The British Empire, the dissolution of which Churchill announced he had no intention of presiding over, is not of transcendent importance in the global scheme of things.

Meanwhile the Cold War that followed the destruction of the Axis Powers in World War II has ended; the Berlin Wall and the Iron Curtain have been dismantled, and East and West Germany have resumed existence as a single nation. In effect the economic and cultural malaise that surfaced in the late nineteenth century, reached crisis proportions in 1914, and thereafter for some eight decades divided the Western world into opposing armed camps, has finally resolved itself. This is not to say, of course, that there will not be new crises, but these are likely to be of a different sort and draw upon different alignments of forces.

Over the course of that eighty-year period there were various switches in national allegiance, but the one abiding tie throughout the entire time was that between Great Britain and the United States. However tardy the U.S. may have been in entering both wars, and despite momentary divergences such as the Suez affair in 1956, there has been a continuity in cultural, social, and, in the last analysis, political outlook that has been as deep-seated as it has been pervasive. Its existence was demonstrated again during the Falkland Islands episode of 1982.

What has happened, however, is that Great Britain's status within what Churchill called "the English-speaking peoples" has changed from one of senior partner, to co-equal, and then to subordinate. At the close of the first decade of the twentieth century, the British Empire seemed to be at its grandest—an island kingdom of some 38,000,000 exercising economic and political suzereignty over an empire of some 350,000,000 constituting a quarter of the world's population. But the head start in industrialization and the political stability that had enabled Britain to establish and maintain its empire had ceased to provide the necessary competitive edge. Not only were other empires being carved out, but the natives were getting increasingly restless.

At least from the days of the Boer War onward, the evidence that the Empire was in trouble was there to read. The transformation in relative importance was taking shape throughout the period 1880–1914; the First World War made it obvious; the Second World War confirmed it; and the decades of the Cold War completed the process. Colonial empires have not coped very well over the past half-century, and without the wealth of a colonial empire to sustain it, the United Kingdom was unable to retain its position. Militarily, economically, and to a certain extent culturally—though, and this is important, *not* for the high culture—the United States has become by far the more powerful partner.

IV

To appreciate the effect of the above upon certain young Englishmen of right-wing persuasion, it is important to keep in mind that this shrinkage of wealth and power took place at the same time that the British ruling class was losing its hegemony over government and finance. Although undeniably facets of the class system still remain, the period from the First World War onward has seen a formidable democratization of British life. As David Cannadine demonstrates in *The Decline and Fall of the British Aristocracy* (1990), the old British establishment's control was far more massive than that in any other European nation, and its erosion thus all the more traumatic. "Between 1880 and 1914, the world that [young British patricians] had been brought up to dominate and to control had emphatically turned against them. And between 1914 and 1918, it was turned completely upside-down."

World War II and the Labour government put the finishing touches on the transaction. To quote Cannadine, "In the world of Wilson and Callaghan, Heath and Foot, public life in Britain was less aristocratic than it had been in the days of Attlee. And in the rampantly petty-bourgeois world of Thatcher, where self-made men are her ideal, the old territorial class appears—with very few exceptions—at best anachronistic and at worst plain irrelevant."

What all this meant was that wealth, education, and family connections no longer provided automatic entreé and status, whether for a young gentleman or, as often happens, a young scion of the middle class equipped with a university education and covetous of rising to privileged station. Indeed, for the latter it is likely to be an especially dismaying business. To have worked so hard to attain elevation to the establishment, and then to find that it no longer runs the show! It is like sneaking under what looked like a circus tent, only to find that a revival is going on inside.

Is it any wonder, then, that a young English academic historian of Tory sentiments and loyalties, entering upon a career at a time when the Cold War drew to an end and a realization of the diminished status of Britain seemed to coincide with the greatly reduced status of the old establishment, might look around for a target, a scapegoat upon which to heap all one's resentment of the lowered expectations and worsened estate? And that, having no personal memories of what Churchill called his countrymen's "finest hour" and reviewing what happened from a perspective dominated by dissatisfaction at the diminished present, he would find precisely that target in the person of the statesman who led his country at the time of greatest peril, and who did indeed, however unwillingly, "preside over the dissolution of the British Empire"? That in fact it had been going on at an accelerating pace for more than a half-century before Churchill became prime minister was irrelevant. To adapt a Latin tag, *post hoc, ergo propter hoc*—Churchill was in place when the mortgage came due; therefore he was to blame for borrowing the money.

It is this frame of mind that accounts for the emotional fervor which seems to be producing not only John Charmley's indictment of Churchill and his earlier apologia for Neville Chamberlain and his umbrella diplomacy, but a spate of revisionist works of history calling into question the values and assumptions on which the conduct of British affairs were based during the greater part of the twentieth century.

Not surprisingly, there has been an attempt to refurbish the tarnished reputations of those historical figures such as Chamberlain and Lord Halifax who, whether by intention or general debility of spirit, sought to delay or to avoid coming to grips with the menace of Nazi Germany. Andrew Roberts's biography of Halifax, *The Holy Fox* (1991), for example, depicts that sad-eyed temporizing Tory as a much-maligned statesman: "it was largely due to his unceasing efforts for peace that Britain could enter the war as the champion of wronged and outraged Civilization"!

It was also due to Halifax and his associates that every effort to stop Hitler before he could play havoc with that Civilization was thwarted, and that anyone who desired to do so was resolutely kept out of office. It was Halifax who visited the Third Reich in 1936 and made it quite clear to Hitler himself that Great Britain had no objections to the *Anschluss* of Austria, the dismemberment of Czechoslovakia, and the enforced annexation of Danzig. Some "champion of wronged and outraged Civilization"!

There has also been an effort to rehabilitate Hitler's Germany itself, to suggest that, while of course its excesses are to be deplored, it was not really as monstrous as depicted, and after all, it *was* dedicated to defeating communism. (Either that, or the revisionist simply glides over the matter. Charmley, for example, can publish a biography of Churchill running to 300,000+ words without having anything to say about Dachau, Auschwitz, Treblinka, etc.) By refusing to seek an accommodation with Hitler, Churchill and Franklin D. Roosevelt only made things worse for the Jews, Poles, and other victims of Nazi conquest. Besides, if left alone Hitler would have concentrated his aggressive impulses on the *Untermenschen* of Eastern Europe. After all, the *Führer* really admired the English. Didn't he say so himself on several occasions?

And so on. I recently read a book by yet another young British historian which advanced the thesis that it was really France, and not Imperial Germany and Austria-Hungary, that was most to blame for causing the First World War! It seems that the French had never accepted the enforced cession of Alsace and Lorraine to Germany after the Franco-Prussian War of 1870, and were so bent upon recovering them that they saw the crisis over Serbia as an opportunity to get Germany involved in a two-front war. They thus encouraged the Russians to begin mobilization, knowing that once that was under way the Germans would have to begin hostilities in order to fend off an attack on themselves and their Austro-Hungarian allies.

It follows that the British, through having already entered into an agreement to coordinate their military and naval plans with France, were much to blame for the advent of the war, because they allowed themselves to get into the position of having a moral obligation to come to the aid of France if the Germans attacked. Thus the French felt safe in taking on the Germans.

It is true, of course, that France did very much want Alsace and Lorraine back, but there is little evidence to validate the theory that she was willing to go to war in order to recover them. On the contrary, French public opinion in 1914 was strongly against war. But if one is going to revise history in order to find a culprit for the decline of the British Empire, why stop with Winston Churchill alone? Why not go back and rewrite the events leading up to 1914?

V

The nub of the revisionist argument is that if Britain had made peace with Hitler, whether before or after the Battle of Britain, the British Empire would have remained intact and the post-1945 Communist domination of Eastern Europe and the Cold War would not have happened. What can one say to such hindsight? The idea that in order to be able to concentrate Germany's full resources on his true heart's desire, the destruction of Soviet Russia, Adolf Hitler sincerely wanted peace, is undoubtedly correct—provided that what is meant by "peace" is understood.

Given Hitler's temperament and ambitions, "peace" on such terms would have consisted of a period of a few years during which the *Wehrmacht* thoroughly crushed the Soviet Union, paused to recuperate, and then proceeded to take care of the British. Indeed, Hitler himself said as much; as Matthew Cooper notes in *The German Army, 1933–1945* (1978), at a conference with his generals on July 31, 1940, the Nazi dictator told them that "decisive victory could be achieved only by the defeat of Britain, but this might be brought about by elimination of the Soviet Union, which, together with the neutralization of the United States by the power of Japan, would end all hope for the little island."

What the approach omits, for one thing, is the nature of the war lord that Hitler aspired to be and was. The notion that such a person, having crushed Russia and made himself master of the continent of Europe and much of Asia, would have been sated, and willing thereafter to coexist peaceably with Great Britain, flies in the face of several thousand years of recorded behavior on the part of military conquerors. When one victory is achieved and one nation subdued, the war lord looks around for another target. Each specified objective is at bottom no more than a means to permit a war to be waged. Why, for example, did Bonaparte choose to renew hostilities against England within two years after signing the Treaty of Amiens in 1802? He had achieved all his supposed objectives, extended the boundaries of France beyond those of the *ancien régime,* regained the overseas colonies seized by the British, secured the recognition of the crowned houses of Europe. There was no real economic or political logic to Napoleon's decision to recommence war. The warfare itself, the winning of victories on battlefields, was what he coveted.

In the same way, in order to unleash his armies, Adolf Hitler invented the pretexts for his wars. As the *Führer* himself put it in 1943, "I am no ordinary soldier-king but a war lord—probably the most successful in history." If there is any hard evidence that he intended to stop finding pretexts to permit military onslaughts, no one has ever produced it. (As for what he would have done with the atomic bomb, on which his scientists were at work in the early 1940s, one shudders to think.)

The belief that because Hitler was bent upon attacking the Soviet Union, he should have been left to do so, and that the Nazi and Communist regimes would then have proceeded to exhaust each other's military might in a protracted war fought in Eastern Europe, is of course cherished by revisionists. It is an example of wishful looking-back at its most glittering. (I should note here that John Charmley does not himself advance this particular argument itself. One gets the idea, however, from what he has to say about the Russians later on, that he would certainly not quarrel with the notion.)

Historically it presupposes that Great Britain could be certain that a German assault on the Soviet Union would turn into a knockdown, drag-out affair that would be exhausting to conqueror and conquered alike. But in 1940 and 1941 that was scarcely a permissible assumption. What with the overwhelming success of the Nazi *blitzkrieg* in Poland in 1939 and in Norway, France, and the Low Countries in 1940, as contrasted with the abysmal performance of the Red Army against Finland in 1939–1940, the probability of a rapid German conquest of the Soviet Union, at relatively little cost in manpower and equipment, was quite high. That Churchill and his military advisers could have foreseen the massive resistance that Russia was able to put up, and the ensuing three-and-a-half-year bloodletting, is most unlikely.

"Barbarossa," the German onslaught against Russia, was three-pronged: a northern thrust aimed at Leningrad, a central thrust through White Russia against Minsk, Smolensk, and ultimately

Moscow, and a southern thrust through the Ukraine toward the Crimea and the Caucasus. Hitler's generals urged him to give primacy to the drive on Moscow, rather than to throw badly needed divisions and equipment into the drive southward. They reasoned that to capture Moscow would not only give them possession of the Soviet Union's political, economic, and military center and the heavy industrial facilities around and to the east of the capital, but by destroying the center of the Russian communications system bring about a virtual paralysis of the enemy's ability to resist effectively. Hitler, however, refused to give priority to the capture of Moscow until too late in the summer, and then was unwilling to divert forces from the southern front to augment the attack. Even so, German spearheads eventually reached within ten miles of Moscow.

Had the *Wehrmacht* been able to use in the Barbarossa offensive even as many as half of the fifty-one divisions and equipment then deployed in Western Europe, and had the *Luftwaffe* been freed from the need to defend against British air attacks on the cities of Germany, it is quite likely that there would have been ample forces to take Moscow and to drive on to eliminate much of the heavy industry located beyond it. As Cooper points out in *The German Army, 1933–1945,* "If the advancing armies could achieve the line Leningrad-Moscow-Rostov before the winter [of 1941–1942] made further movement impossible, before the divisions from the Far East could move west, and before the Soviet mobilization machinery could produce too many field divisions, victory would indeed be possible."

So the fact that when Hitler invaded the Soviet Union, the British, though without a bridgehead on the continent, were still very much in the war and tying down almost one-fourth of the *Wehrmacht's* divisions and no small portion of the German air force clearly had a formidable impact upon the German failure to destroy the Soviet Union's powers of resistance in the swift, lethal campaign that Barbarossa was meant to be. Thus the hypothesis that Great Britain could have made peace and then allowed the German and Soviet war machines to wear each other out in Eastern Europe will not stand up to scrutiny.

VI

If. . . . It is so tempting to isolate a single factor, a single action not taken or decision not made, without regard to its full historical context, and to say that if only this or that had been done, all would have turned out differently. The assumption is that whatever else happened both before and afterwards would have stayed in place unchanged. But history doesn't work that way. One action causes a compensating action, which in turn results in another, and so on.

Even if it is assumed that Hitler would have been willing to allow Great Britain to go its own way once the Soviet Union had been conquered and subdued, which is a very great deal to assume, is it likely that a humiliated and demoralized United Kingdom could have held onto its overseas possessions for very long? What would have been the response of Canada to England's knuckling under? Would it have remained a loyal part of the British Empire? What would have happened when the Japanese moved upon the British territories and possessions in southeast Asia? And what of India? Would it have been content to stay quiescent?

How long would the Suez Canal, that vital link between the United Kingdom and its overseas possessions, have stayed under British control? Britain was also engaged in a war with Benito Mussolini's Fascist Italy. It is true that the Italian army had shown little aptitude for desert warfare in North Africa, and Germany had been forced to send an Afrika Korps to its rescue. But that Hitler would have stood by for very long once the Duce renewed his designs upon the British protectorates in North Africa and the Middle East seems improbable.

Moreover, the Spain of Francisco Franco, emboldened by Britain's acquiescence and with Hitler's encouragement and blessing, would surely have demanded the cession of Gibraltar. How long, therefore, would the Mediterranean Sea have remained open to the British navy and to British commerce? And how long would it have been before the industrial might of a victorious Germany, able now to draw upon the full resources of a conquered Europe, created a *Luftwaffe* of overpowering strength and a submarine fleet that could erase British shipping from the high seas?

What then of the great Empire that a peace agreement with Adolf Hitler supposedly would have been saved for Britain? Every likelihood is that it would have commenced to disintegrate almost at once, and the more so because, peace agreement or no peace peace agreement, Britain could not have dared to employ its fleet and its resources elsewhere in the face of even the possibility of a cross-channel invasion by the Germans.

Lastly, what would have been the impact, politically and psychologically, of such a pact with Nazi Germany upon Great Britain itself? What would have been its effect upon the tradition of free speech, individual liberties, religious freedom, minority rights, and democratic government that, for all the lingering class system that still marked English society, had evolved over the course of 500 years of immunity from foreign invasion? Would England have remained the England that we knew, and that we know today?

To put the question another way, could the England that we knew, the England of Winston Churchill, ever have consented, once engaged in a war, to accept a peace treaty dictated by Nazi Germany? To contend that it ought to have done so, that it was in its long-range economic interests to have done so, is, finally, irrelevant.

Churchill had come to power, after his long years of political banishment, precisely because he embodied the national determination to stand up to the threat that Hitler's Germany constituted to British freedom. The evasions, moral compromises, and submissions of the 1930s were over. To suggest that the people of England—as distinguished, perhaps, from the old men of the Conservative Party—would have been willing to acquiesce in what would obviously be a humiliating, craven settlement while that menace still existed, is to misread the times, the place, and the people.

In his biographical put-down of Britain's wartime leader, Charmley spends considerable effort in developing the point that in 1945 Churchill ended up acquiescing in Russian control of Poland, which he depicts as making a hypocrisy and travesty of Churchill's insistence upon combating Germany for attacking Poland in 1939—the implication being that in not wishing to stop Hitler, the appeasers were justified. As if there were no distinction to be made between a response to the naked and unprovoked aggression of Nazi Germany, and to the actions, however ruthless, taken to create a postwar defensive buffer of satellite states by a wartime ally whose borders had been invaded, cities devastated, and twenty million of whose citizenry had perished!

The creation of the Iron Curtain in 1945–1947, for all its potentiality for flare-ups, was basically a defensive measure. The Soviet Union's essential strategy in the ensuing Cold War was to move in where it could, but to stop short of war. It could be, and was finally, "contained." Hitler's Germany, by contrast, had only one posture: military conquest, and no strategy of containment could have worked for very long.

I noted earlier that Charmley is able to equate Hitler's domination of Europe during World War II with America's postwar economic and political hegemony. While to be subjected to the latter is "certainly preferable," the difference between the two is supposedly one of degree rather than of kind. With equal logic, one might say that having a wisdom tooth removed is "certainly preferable" to castration.

VII

It is Charmley's contention that the great error of Winston Churchill's thinking was his sentimental reliance upon the United States of America and its president, Franklin D. Roosevelt. In so arguing, he offers a picture of the American scene during the early years of the war that is difficult for one who actually remembers the period to recognize. I quote a representative comment: "Despite the Churchillian legend, to which American participants in the war were only too happy to pay lip-service later, there was no widespread desire in June or July 1940 to help the British."

To students of twentieth-century American history, this will come as a considerable surprise. Certainly there was an articulate Isolationist contingent in the nation, particularly in the Midwest, and there would have been little support for entering the war as a belligerent at the time. But public opinion was overwhelmingly on the side of Britain; an opinion poll taken in July 1940 indicated that seven out of ten Americans believed that a Nazi victory would place the United States in danger, and so were in favor of assistance to the embattled British. Despite the parlous condition of American arms, the War Department turned over extensive stocks of surplus or outdated arms, munitions, and aircraft to Britain. In the month of June alone, more than $43,000,000 worth of supplies were dispatched across the Atlantic. It wasn't much, but it was all the United States had; as late as a year later, America's own expanding armed forces were conducting maneuvers with make-believe weapons because the available equipment had been sent to England the summer before. Charmley to the contrary notwithstanding, the retrospective judgment of an operative in the German *Abwehr* military counter-intelligence service, that "In the year 1940, America saved England," is, though overstated, a more accurate summation of what the president and a large majority of the American people desired.

The United States, after all, was *not* at war with Germany in 1940, and Roosevelt was being savagely assailed by his opponents as a warmonger who if reelected would surely plunge the nation into war. The power to declare war was vested in Congress, not the president. What Roosevelt was able and willing to do under the circumstances seems, in retrospect, quite remarkable. If there were times when even a desperate Winston Churchill expressed exasperation at the seeming tardiness of the American response to what he perceived as the common danger, most reputable historians of the period would rate Roosevelt's efforts to support an embattled Britain as highly effective.

The fact that Americans in general, including Roosevelt, had no great admiration for Great Britain's far-flung Empire as such is another matter; when it came down to the question of England versus Nazi Germany, there was little doubt of where U.S. sympathies lay. Otherwise Roosevelt would not have been able to do what he did.

Without question the United States profited from the sale of arms, aircraft, munitions, and other material of war to Britain, and just as in World War I, it emerged from the conflict in far better economic condition than did its allies. The effect of England's involvement in the two wars was to bring it close to bankruptcy. The task of standing up to the enemies of the free world is an expensive business, as the United States subsequently discovered during the Cold War. Moreover, like the United States, Britain now confronts the ironic fact that the two countries that were the principal enemies, Germany and Japan, have emerged from the long ordeal in highly prosperous condition, having been spared the expense of maintaining the military deterrent to Soviet expansion. This is very much a part of the dissatisfaction prompting the revisionist impulse, and understandably so. (I've no doubt that as the memory of the Berlin Airlift and the Korean War fades, the revisionists of a future era will be demonstrating that the defense of the West and the containment of the Soviet Union were quite unnecessary, and the North Atlantic Treaty Organization a waste of time and money. Indeed, the partisans of the New Left, in their zeal to attack our Vietnam involvement, were already saying as much in the late 1960s and 1970s.)

There is no point in taking up all of John Charmley's arguments in deflation of what he considers the "Churchill Myth." The basic thrust of the biography is that Churchill was a romantic Victorian whose egocentricity was exceeded only by his ambition. He is granted precious few statesmanly virtues. Even the notion that the reason why Churchill wanted, in 1943 and 1944, to carry the war into the Balkans was to prevent the advancing Russians from dominating all of Eastern and Central Europe is scouted. If Charmley is to be believed, Churchill had no such foresight, for he almost never took the long-range view of anything. His decisions were based on love of adventure and military audacity, not on rational calculation. The wartime prime minister comes off as a cross between Harry Hotspur and Don Quixote.

That the world, and in particular the Western world, would have been a more comfortable place to live in if it had managed to remain at peace can scarcely be doubted. The cost exacted by the failure of human beings to be wiser and more peaceable than they proved to be—close to 100,000,000 dead, untold billions of dollars spent on the materiel for killing them—is appalling to contemplate. Yet to single out a particular event during that time, a specific decision, and to say that if only it hadn't happened, or had happened differently, then all or most of the catastrophe could have been avoided, is a profitless undertaking. And to contend that individuals of good will, finding themselves caught up in that terrible happening, could or should have declined to stand up to both the immediate and the long-range threat posed to themselves, their countries, and all that they believed in, is to acquiesce in the very barbarity and destructiveness itself. It was indeed a time when, in the poet Yeats' words, "The best lack all conviction, while the worst / Are full of passionate intensity." Fortunately there was a Winston Churchill who saw what was at stake.

It is so tempting to look back at the eight decades of hot and cold war, and to try to argue that the whole wretched business was not worth the effort. But in essence what the argument amounts to is a fond wish that the twentieth century hadn't happened, that not only the war against Hitler's Germany but that against the Kaiser's Germany as well had never taken place, and that somewhere around the globe, for twenty-four hours of each day the sun still shone upon the Union Jack. Ernest Hemingway's character Jake Barnes provides the proper answer for this at the conclusion of *The Sun Also Rises:* "Isn't it pretty to think so?"

If one is a young Briton of relatively limited expectations who feels deprived of proper status and forced to make one's way in a plebeian world, it must indeed be pretty to think that it could and should all have happened differently, that by rights the Empire should still be intact, with Britannia continuing to rule the waves and the pre-1914 establishment still in control of government. But it didn't happen that way, and scolding one's elders for standing up to Nazi Germany in 1940 will not bring back either the British Empire or the Garden of Eden.

(1994)

Sir William at the Hot Gates

The death last summer of Sir William Golding in England at the age of eighty-one brought back to memory a piquant example of the workings of the creative imagination that the Nobel laureate once provided. I like to think of it as a prime demonstration of the way that prosaic fact, if properly expanded upon, can be made to offer striking human insight.

When Golding and his wife, Ann, arrived at Hollins College, Virginia, in September of 1961, to begin a year as writer-in-residence, his *Lord of the Flies* had only recently appeared in American paperback and was rapidly becoming a best-seller on college and university campuses. Not long afterward I had agreed to represent a learned society at the inauguration of a new chancellor at the College of William and Mary, and since the Goldings had not seen central or eastern Virginia, I invited them to come along.

To get from Hollins, in western Virginia, to Williamsburg—this was in the days before interstate highways—one drove east from Roanoke on U.S. 460 to a point eighteen miles beyond Lynchburg, then turned north on a state highway over to U.S. 60, and thence to Richmond and on to Williamsburg. My parents lived in Richmond, and I had made the drive so many times that I no longer thought about what might be viewed en route, but only in terms of getting where I was going.

The speed limit in Virginia then was 50 mph. It was important to drive at or near it when on 460, for there was a state police headquarters east of Lynchburg and the road was well patrolled. Once having turned off and headed north, however, one could drive considerably faster, for the state road between 460 and 60 was seldom if ever patrolled. When I drove east with the Goldings, therefore, I stayed on the speed limit while on 460, then, when I reached the turnoff, stepped on the gas.

A couple of miles north of the turnoff is the McLean House, where General Robert E. Lee surrendered the Army of Northern Virginia to General U. S. Grant in 1865. As we went speeding by, I was reminded of its presence by a road sign and several cannon along the highway, and I pointed it out to the Goldings.

They began laughing. I was puzzled, until they explained that they thought it funny that I, a southerner, was racing past the scene of the Confederate surrender at 65 mph. But I had passed by it many times before, and my thoughts were not on Lee's failure to elude Grant but on my own chances for avoiding state troopers.

We drove on to Richmond, spent the night there, toured Williamsburg and Jamestown the next day, I took part in the inaugural procession, and we returned to Roanoke. Nothing of other than a casual nature was said about the War between the States.

At the time Golding was writing essays for a British magazine, the *Spectator*. These were collected in a book, *The Hot Gates*, published four years later in 1965. What was my surprise, upon reading that book, to find the trip to Williamsburg recorded there—in, however, creatively enhanced format.

In a piece entitled "Fable," about the underlying theme of *Lord of the Flies*, Golding was discoursing upon the workings of that "force which we call history, and how uncontrollable that force is even among the most detached of men." To illustrate this, the drive to Williamsburg became a tour of the Civil War battlefields of Virginia. Throughout the tour his host, "a Southerner and a scholar," had provided a quite objective, nonpartisan account of the war, but as the day wore on "his voice began to return to his origins."

What had been a balanced, unbiased exposition delivered "at a discreet 40 miles an hour" grew more passionate as the last maneuver of Lee was countered by Grant. "His voice had lost all pretence of scholarship. . . . When we came to Appomattox, this educated and indeed rather cynical man grunted, 'Aw, shucks!' and drove past the place where Lee surrendered to Grant at seventy-five miles an hour." (Note the 10 mph increase in speed.)

Thus, although he was supposedly writing journalistic nonfiction, Golding's storytelling imagination had converted a practical response to the absence of state troopers and radar sets into a demonstration of the force of historical atavism. That the actual motivation had nothing to do with the defeat of the Confederacy, and that it was Golding who was supplying the causative link, is unimportant. The "probable impossible" was once again shown to be superior to the historical fact for the purposes of truth-telling.

The story does not end there. For now that the lily of actuality had been sufficiently gilded by the creative imagination, it had become available for purposes of scientific analysis. Thus three years later appeared a book entitled *Brain Storms: A Study of Human Spontaneity* by Wayne Barker, M.D. (1968). In it Barker, a neuropsychiatrist, sets out to analyze "those sudden whirlwinds of spontaneous activity by which the brain copes with threats to the continuity of our everyday living." What should turn up there but the selfsame incident, which, thanks to Golding's creative imagination, could now be used to illuminate the murky transaction between physiological and psychological response.

As Dr. Barker sees it, the struggle to maintain "the role of detached, objective scholar by dissociating regional emotionalism required increasing tension. Prodromal signs warn of an impending crisis. His speech begins to shift from academic to Southern. Emotion creeps in. Immediate warning signs appear when his scholarly pose falters, pressure on the accelerator increases, and the car begins to move faster. At Appomattox, the grunt, 'Aw, shucks!' is not unlike some of the verbal cries that immediately precede convulsions. But instead of a convulsive fit, he falls silent, presses hard on the gas, and speeds away."

Thus the future Sir William's creative enlargement of what were tactics designed to deal with the radar weapons of the Virginia State Highway Patrol made possible first a discourse on the emotional force of historical loyalties, and then a psychiatric explanation by Dr. Barker of what can cause highway wrecks. "How many traffic violations are set off by similar reactions equally deserving of the designation fit?"

How many indeed? And how many sizzling fits of scientific creativity are likewise set off by the imaginative observation of supposed phenomena that, in the cold light of later and closer scrutiny, turn out not to be phenomena at all? I did not read all of Wayne Barker's discourse on brain storms and human spontaneity, but I hope that his premises rest upon sterner evidence than the example that William Golding had to offer.

As for what Bill Golding had made of it, well, he had a way of taking stands based upon how he thought things should be. Later that school year I saw this demonstrated very nicely. *Lord of the Flies* was by then all the rage; everywhere he went he was bombarded with questions about the meaning and the symbolism of this or that. Yet the British tradition of amateurism then prescribed that good novelists and poets are not supposed to think, or have thought, abstractly or theoretically about what they have written. It is all done intuitively; the storyteller tells the story, and it is up to the critic, the pedant, to figure out the intricacies and patterns of its meanings. Golding didn't know what all the symbolism of *Lord of the Flies* meant. No indeed. This talk of symbols and linked meanings was beyond his ken.

That year I was teaching a course in the twentieth-century novel, and I thought it would be appropriate to take up *Lord of the Flies*. On the day we discussed it, there was considerable argument in the class. One very literal-minded male graduate student from the Midwest raised all kinds of objections, developed an extensive theoretical paraphrasing, and the like. This particular young man came under the rubric of Louis Armstrong's formulation to this effect: "There's some people that if they don't already know, there's no use trying to tell 'em." Even so I decided to let the class have a crack at the author himself, and vice versa, and I invited Golding to attend the next meeting.

I prefaced the occasion by explaining that although Golding might be said to possess an informed opinion about the workings of his novel, now that the novel had been published, he occupied no privileged position with respect to it. Then I threw the session open to questions.

As I expected, at the outset Bill professed to have little or no notion as to the various meanings being discovered in his novel. He was just a plain old-fashioned storyteller, etc. (in much the same way that William Faulkner professed to be just a plain old unsophisticated country boy who just happened to write *The Sound and the Fury*.) Presently, however, as the students—or, more properly, as the particular literal-minded male graduate student from the Midwest began to develop his own elaborate reading of what Bill had written, Golding swiftly abandoned his pose of standoffishness. He quoted chapter and verse, pointed out relationships, made it quite evident that not only did he know exactly what was in his novel, but that whatever he put in it was placed there to serve a specific purpose. Authoritatively he undercut the graduate student's facile schematization. Nobody was going to take unwarranted liberties with the novel *he* had written.

In short the "just plain storyteller" approach was all right, so long as nobody took undue liberties with what he had written. But, when that happened, Golding dropped it forthwith, and proceeded to demonstrate what now must surely be obvious to anyone who has ever read *Lord of the Flies*—that his book was the product of an author who was possessed of a formidable analytical intelligence, capable of developing the most careful and intricate thematic dimensions in a work of fiction. Nothing was in the novel that didn't belong there. At all points the author's creative imagination functioned in close concert with his critical intelligence.

Golding's art, especially in the four early novels of which *Lord of the Flies* was one, consisted in just that creative alliance between the inventive and the analytical; he was, in an original way, a prime representative of that long-established English tradition of the Novel of Ideas, from Swift and *Rasselas* onward. He saw things in terms of the linkages between them, and he wrote stories that were designed from the outset to demonstrate the way that things were.

The little incident of the supposed battlefield tour remains for me a convincing example of what can happen when seemingly mundane fact is conducted through the hot gates of the creative imagination. It is also additional evidence, if any were needed, of why in 1983 Sir William Golding was awarded the Nobel Prize for Literature.

(1994)

Literature and the Great War

The newspaper in Scotland, where we were vacationing this past summer, contained a lengthy feature story, telling of the death of the writer's youthful uncle seventy-five years earlier, on July 1, 1916, the first day of the Battle of the Somme. Meanwhile the television news was showing sequences from the current crisis in the Balkans, involving Serbia, Slovenia, Bosnia, Herzegovina, placenames that had not figured in international discourse since the summer that the archduke was assassinated.

Bosnia? Herzegovina? My god! To remember the outbreak of the Great War—World War I—and the Battle of the Somme with any clarity, one would have to be in one's mid-eighties. And to be old enough to have served in the A.E.F.—the American Expeditionary Force—one would be in one's nineties. Of the almost five million Americans who were in the armed forces in 1917–1918, according to the *World Almanac*, fewer than 90,000 were still alive last year. Xerxes of Persia, gazing down from a hilltop upon the vast array of men and ships engaged in crossing the Hellespont, is said by Herodotus to have wept at the thought that in a hundred years not one person of all the mighty host lying below him would still be alive. "Pack up your troubles in your old kit bag and smile, smile, smile!"

It is said that writing about wars customarily adheres to a pattern. For a decade or so after a war ends, there is much reader inter-

est. The major figures write their memoirs, and the returned veterans are eager to read about their own experience in the larger context of the fighting. Then topical interest wanes, and for several
decades most books on the subject attract little notice and only professional military people and a few historians continue to concern
themselves with what happened.

When the former rank-and-file of the armies and navies reach
late middle age, retire from their civilian jobs and vocations, and
begin looking back, a resurgence of interest develops. The fact, so
long taken for granted, that one was involved, when young, in an
extraordinary and momentous activity, given a uniform and transported to strange places, and, if sent into combat, made to partici-
pate in shocking events and endure all manner of discomforts and
ordeals, becomes in later life an occasion for wonder. The memoirs
again appear in droves, this time not by the major figures but by
the onetime rank-and-file. Meanwhile passions have receded, the
military historians revaluate command performances, and the battles and campaigns, strategy and tactics, come in for renewed and
more nearly objective scrutiny. Thereafter interest in and study of
a war becomes a matter of pure historical involvement alone.

In the instance of World War I, however, there *was* no "third
stage," or at most a very muted version of it, for during the 1950s
and 1960s, when the veterans of 1914–1918 had reached their time of
retrospection, the Second World War had intervened—a greater and
more far-reaching event (especially for the United States) with more
momentous and terrible consequences. The results of 1914–1918 had
proved to be neither decisive nor lasting; and from a standpoint of
getting books written and published, few persons there were who
wished to read about the Somme, Ypres, Tannenburg, Jutland, Passchendaele, and the Meuse-Argonne.

So the Great War's veterans went to their graves without their
latter-day revival; no fifty-years-later festivals of onetime mortal foes
shaking hands across the formerly muddy and louse-infested

trenches, no sentimental journeys to St. Mihiel and Flanders Field, no reenactments of Zeppelin raids or mustard-gas attacks. Behind the thought of Paul von Hindenburg and his *pickelhaube* lay one's consciousness of Adolf Hitler, the swastika, and the gas ovens. When Scott Fitzgerald had his narrator in *The Great Gatsby* refer to the Great War as a "delayed Teutonic migration," he was essentially correct. Thwarted in 1918, the Fatherland thereafter dropped all pretense of being civilized, and reverted to the diplomatic tactics and social attitudes of Attila the Hun.

Chronologically speaking, a scholar writing about 1914–1918 today bears much the same relationship to General John J. Pershing and the A.E.F. as Theodore Roosevelt did to Oliver Hazard Perry and the sail-powered navy when he was writing *A Naval History of the War of 1812* in the early 1880s. He can be objective enough about the performance of American arms to describe ineptitude without apology or alibi. It is quite possible for a historian like Colonel Rod Paschall to point out that despite the extremely low number of American casualties in the Great War as compared with those of England, France, and Germany, the deaths and wounding suffered by the A.E.F. were extraordinarily high in relation to the period of actual involvement in combat and the number of troops engaged (*The Defeat of Imperial Germany, 1917–1918.* 1989). American leadership had failed to benefit from the four-year experience of the British and French on the Western Front, and was basing U.S. tactics on advance by concentrated rifle fire, as if the machine guns hadn't discouraged that approach for several years. At Belleau Wood in 1918 the U.S. Marine brigade was sent charging right into the teeth of machine gun fire, advancing four deep in human-wave attacks after the fashion of 1914, or, for that matter, of Grant's army at Cold Harbor in 1864. German and British observers, seeing the American dead fallen in serried rows in the Argonne Forest, expressed admiration for their courage and severe criticism of their tactical leadership. (American casualties totalled 364,800, as compared with more than nine million Russians killed, wounded, missing, or captured, six million French, seven million Germans, seven million Austro-Hungarians, three million English and Commonwealth troops, and two million Italians.)

Colonel Paschall's revaluation of what happened during the final two years of the Great War involves a marked upgrading of the leadership on the Western Front. He does not see such figures as Douglas Haig, who commanded the British armies from 1916 onward, as stupid, unimaginative, unfeeling old martinets who knew no better than repeatedly to dispatch entire brigades and divisions of men over the top and straight into the face of machine guns and artillery barrages. The offensive tactics that early in World War II sent the German *blitzkrieg* hurtling through France and the Low Countries and almost trapped the British at Dunkirk, and that in 1944 and 1945 enabled Eisenhower's invading forces to hurl Hitler's armies back across the Rhine, were all developed by the generals of the Great War, who, however, possessed neither the resources nor the equipment to employ them successfully. In Paschall's summation, "in reality, most World War II leaders simply repeated what they had seen implemented under the direction of Foch, Pétain, Haig, Sims, Trenchard, and Ludendorff. There would not be much new in World War II; the changes were already in motion during 1917."

Yet if the war of 1939–1945 was vaster, more destructive, and more far-reaching in scope than that of 1914–1918, it is nonetheless true that in terms of cultural shock and the imaginative impact on life in the Western world, the Great War came on with greater and more decisive impress. There were numerous reasons for this. Except for the American Civil War, and then only in the southern states, there had been no extended all-out wars involving large segments of the civilian population for a full century. During that time the available weaponry had benefitted enormously in deadliness from the Industrial Revolution. A greatly more destructive and more impersonal kind of warfare, coming as it did after a hundred years of relative peace in Europe, happened to a population that by 1914 was constituted largely of citizens who were literate, who could read and compare versions of what was told to them, and who voted. It came after a century of material improvement and prosperity, which was paralleled by a political and philosophical idealism that called for things to get better and better, and that elevated love of country to the status of belief in God and devotion to Truth and Beauty.

The shock of trench warfare—the appalling, almost suicidal requirements of going over the top against emplaced machine guns, mass slaughter of long-range artillery fired by unseen opponents, the huge scale on which war was being waged—was mind-searing. As the western front settled into a condition of bloody stalemate, the conditions under which men were made to live and to fight seemed the antithesis of what civilized existence was supposed to be. After it became obvious that there would be no quick solution to the ordeal, the moral and ethical assumptions developed during generations of peace and of seeming material and social progress received an abrupt check. The ensuing disillusionment, coming as it did so swiftly and catastrophically, called into question the validity of the basic ideals under which the Western world had supposedly been functioning. The gap between belief and actuality, between patriotic faith and the requirements of trench warfare, took on the dimensions of an abyss.

Paul Fussell, in his widely praised *The Great War and Modern Memory* (1975), has described and interpreted the impress made by the shock of the Great War upon English modes of thought and expression, which in turn, as Fussell demonstrates, influenced American attitudes. Such impress went far beyond the war itself; it permeated, and has continued to permeate, the Western world's ways of seeing the human condition. The key concept for Fussell in his consideration of the impact of 1914–1918 is irony: "I am saying that there seems to be one dominating form of modern understanding; that it is essentially ironic; and that it originates largely in the application of mind and memory to the events of the Great War."

The ironic vision was by no means invented in late 1914 and 1915; Fussell opens with a consideration of Thomas Hardy's poems, which in their perception of incongruity presage the response of poets both English and American to what would soon follow. He then proceeds to demonstrate how the imagery of trench warfare, bombardment, wounds, "combat fatigue," futility, disbelief in the reality of any kind of victory that would be commensurate with the human cost of achieving it, juxtaposed with the patriotic rhetoric, official pronouncements, and pious ideality, suffuses modern consciousness. Fussell discusses the writings of Wilfred Owen, Siegfried Sassoon, Robert Graves, Edmund Blunden, and other British authors; he then develops the continuity of attitude in such authors as Anthony Burgess, Joseph Heller, and Thomas Pynchon.

The Great War and Modern Memory is a thesis book: it develops a psychological point and argues for it. Occasionally the thesis becomes omnivorous—for example, trenches being dug in threes (forward, support, reserve) and other tripartite divisions decreed by the nature of the Great War supposedly fed myth and legend with particular appropriateness. I suspect that just as convincing an argument could be developed for just about any war, any historical period, or any low single-digit number; it was an Ancient Mariner, not a British tommy, who, like a poor-caliber infielder, stoppeth one of three. Yet Fussell's basic thesis—that the impact of the trench warfare of 1914–1918 upon a popular and literary imagination unprepared for its magnitude, impersonal nature, bloodiness, and animality was both devastating and enduring—is imaginatively advanced and soundly demonstrated.

Of a very different nature, but concerned with the literary and cultural ramifications of the same historical event, is Samuel Hynes's book, *A War Imagined: The First World War and English Culture* (1991), Hynes has long since shown himself to be our major student of Edwardian and Georgian English letters. He writes with the authority of the scholar and the insight of the critic, and does not so much develop and argue points as reveal and identify patterns. In *A War Imagined* he examines the way that English writers and painters, as well as sculptors and musicians, dealt with, depicted, and were affected by the First World War, from its beginnings through to the Armistice, and then the postwar years culminating in the General Strike of 1926.

Hynes is at pains to make clear that the notion that the coming of war to Great Britain in 1914 brought a sudden end to a stable, progressive, comfortably ordered and civilized society is a considerable over-simplification—a myth prompted by nostalgia. Ireland was close to a state of civil war at the time; the suffragettes were turning violent; trade unions were threatening a general strike: "a civil war, a sex war, and a class war: in the spring of 1914 these were all foreseen in England's immediate future." On the cultural front the advocates of futurism and vorticism were proclaiming an all-out attack upon the Edwardian "establishment."

When the Great War erupted, Hynes points out, it was identified by older figures such as Edmund Gosse as a potential "disinfectant that would cleanse the present—and not simply present art, but all of 'our' self-indulgent, hedonistic, luxurious habits." Thus Gosse, he says, "could be positive about the situation in France: war would purify and cleanse; war was good for England." Surveying a wide spectrum of writings about the war by various hands on various cultural levels, Hynes shows how "the war against Germany rapidly became a war against Modernism"; war was being declared against the avant-garde. Denunciations of everything German— including German music, German thought, German science, German romanticism—were rampant. Yet as Hynes notes, so much of what was being repudiated had equally been English, and the result was not only a diminishment of English culture but "a further widening of that gap between the past and the present, that breach in the perceived continuity of history, which was the war's most striking legacy to the world after the war."

Yet there *was* dissent, Hynes shows: the Bloomsbury group among others were dissenters even in the early years of the war. What happened, Hynes declares, is that "a divided culture began to emerge: on the one hand, the war culture—patriotic, restrictive, and 'official,' and on the other, that conflux of opposing faiths—the artists, pacifists, women, and radical Christians who constituted such opposition to the war as there was."

The turning point in the way that English writers and artists depicted the war and at least a segment of the general public viewed it, Hynes says, came in 1916, mainly following the huge losses in the Somme offensive. Patriotic idealism, Rupert Brooke–fashion ("If I should die, think only this of me, / that there's some corner of a foreign field / that is forever England . . . "), gave way to a considerably more sardonic view of the waging of war:

> Protests against it began to be heard, both from civilians in high places and from serving soldiers, and a new English war art began to emerge that uttered its own protest simply by recording a new trench reality. That new reality had to do with details that had largely been left out of previous war art: the devastated earth, the corpses, and the wounded—blinded men, gassed men, crippled men, mad men, men with self-inflicted wounds. But it also had to do with feelings that were new to the art of this war: pity and compassion for its victims, anger and hatred for non-combatants.

Hynes traces the forms and shapes of this new art, much of it by and for soldiers, in a series of detailed chapters that authoritatively survey work by representative writers and artists. The war effort continued, and so did the efforts of those who would suppress dissent on the grounds that "pacifists were refusing to serve in the army, and were persuading others to refuse; advocates of a negotiated peace were weakening the nation's resolve to fight on to total victory; and a permissive, un-English decadence in high places was corrupting

English society."

By 1918 what was to be England's "postwar modernism" was beginning to emerge, in the writings of returning soldiers, the Bloomsbury group, dissenters such as D. H. Lawrence, and the like. What had resulted was a sense of deep discontinuity. A work such as Lytton Strachey's *Eminent Victorians*, for example, seemingly had nothing whatever to do with the Great War; yet its demolition of Victorianism was a demonstration that "History was not a story of liberal progress, with a continuous happy ending; the ending was the war. And so the story would have to be re-told to accommodate that disaster." The past was dead, the future all but unimaginable. If English society was to be reconstructed, there could be no postwar return to what in Edwardian England was believed to be the Good, the True, and the Beautiful. What rough beast was slouching its way to Balmoral Castle to be born?

Hynes examines the various models being proposed. He identifies five distinct postwar clusters of literary activity: (1) "The Old Men," the surviving late Victorian elders such as Gosse, Sir Henry Newbolt, etc., who saw the war as a continuation of their prewar values; (2) "Edwardians," such as H. G. Wells and Arnold Bennett, who strove to stay up-to-date but were disturbed and apprehensive about what had been lost and what survived; (3) "The Pre-War Avant-Garde," such as Wyndham Lewis, Ezra Pound, etc., who had declared war on conservative art back before the Great War began, but whose formulations for doing so had thoroughly disintegrated; (4) "The War Generation," or "Lost Generation," including both the surviving soldiers of what had been a massacre of the upper and middle classes, and those who had stayed at home but were likewise disoriented, confused, groping for order—Huxley, Eliot, Muir, Lawrence, Middleton Murry, Woolf, etc.; and (5) "The Post-War Generation," growing into adulthood as and after the war ended— Evelyn Waugh, Ronald Firbank, and so on. The working members of all these groups had to deal with a greatly changed English soci ety and world, marked by a sense of radical discontinuity. Their responses were of numerous kinds.

It would be impractical to attempt further to summarize Hynes's summarization of post-1918 literary England, which is explicit, succinct, and informed; but I cannot refrain from quoting one passage. In it he is looking at the writers who did not serve in the war but who set the tone for dealing with what had happened:

> Eliot and Pound, Virginia Woolf and Lawrence—these are major Modernists, writers whose works define what is most valued in English writings of the 1920s. None of them had any experience of the war, and none wrote a war novel or a war poem in the customary sense of those terms. But they did something more interesting, and perhaps more important: they assimilated the war into their writing, both as concept and as form, made it a part of their idea of history, and of reality. The version of history that they shared is the post-war version; it renders recent history as discontinuous and fragmented, civilization as ruined, the past as lost. . . . Their writings contain no battle scenes, no heroes, and no victories; they pick up from the war only the dominating negative themes—the death of civilization and the loss of Eden, and the negative characters—the damaged victims, and the tyrannous Old Men. And they construct out of this heap of broken images the forms of the history of their own time.

Has anyone ever put that particular point better?

The important literature dealing with the war itself, Hynes notes, did not begin to appear until late in the decade. He sees the ten-day General Strike of 1926 as the event that, culturally, intellectually, and psychologically, "ended" the Great War itself. The strike, which came close to paralyzing the working of British society, was described and thought of as a war against society and, when it was broken, as a victory. Like the war the strike had forced another gap in the continuity of history, Hynes says, and when it was over the events of 1914–1918 were sufficiently distanced in the imagination so that new ideas could now find expression. The Myth of the Great War—that it betrayed the ideals of the past, turned men into victims of an inhuman machine so that they fought for no cause, destroyed the idea of progress, civilization, England, and left the survivors to live among a heap of ruins—now took form in prose, poetry, painting, movies. "The history of English art and thought in the Twenties," Hynes declares, "is a record of attempts to reconstruct history and values, and so build a new culture out of the broken images made by the war. Only at the end of that decade was the war itself remade, the vast loss described and mythologized, in the prose narratives that became the war-book canon."

The effect of all this upon the 1930s is not Hynes's story. He does, however, note that it was this Myth of the War, inherited by the next generation and intensified by the Great Depression, that made the 1930s what they were, including pacifism, political activism, proto-fascism, and the defensive drawing-in when the Western democracies were confronted by the rise of totalitarianism. When World War II came, those who marched off to fight it "would go without dreams of glory, expecting nothing except suffering, boredom and perhaps death—not cynically, but without illusions, because they remembered a war: not the Great War itself, but the Myth that had been made of it."

A War Imagined, it seems to me, has taken a complex cultural entity—the literature written in England over the course of almost two decades, as well as the visual arts, music, film—and examined it in terms of its relationship to a mammoth, near-catastrophic political and social event, the Great War and the decade following it. Hynes has enabled us to see and to understand what the relationship was and what it meant, both for the creative work and the culture from which it rose. For a literary historian who is also a fine critic, I can think of few more useful undertakings.

To my knowledge no one has successfully brought off a similar study of American literature with anything of the scope and range of Sam Hynes's book. Yet, as a British critic noted some years ago, despite the brevity of our involvement, the Great War's impact on the American literary imagination was extraordinarily penetrating and pervasive. And perhaps this is less paradoxical than might appear, for as has often been pointed out, our entrance into the conflict in 1917 ended what until then had been not merely a geographical but a psychological isolation from the Old World. Coinciding as it did with the formal disappearance of the western frontier, the arrival of American troops in France wrote a formal conclusion to the Emersonian dream of regeneration in nature and the creation of a new man free of the bondage and toils of the European past. As one historian, Henry W. May, entitled his study of late nineteenth- and early twentieth-century American society, it was truly *The End of American Innocence*. (To be sure, all of our best novelists—Cooper, Hawthorne, Melville, James, Clemens—had long since discounted any such possibility, but naive optimism dies hard, and three thousand miles of ocean and an open frontier had constituted a powerful temptation.) In any event, whatever the causes, the literary response to the Great War was as marked, and as morose, among American as among English authors.

I want to turn back briefly to Paul Fussell's observation that irony has been the predominant mode of the twentieth-century literary imagination, and that the Great War has significantly to do with that. Has anyone ever thought of the New Criticism as constituting an oblique response to the War of 1914–1918? Sam Hynes suggests as much, when he cites Laura Riding's and Robert Graves's *A Survey of Modernist Poetry,* published in 1927, as not only the first book to use the term *modernist* to identify avant-garde writing, but "the first to demonstrate a new critical method for dealing with Modernist texts—the method that would come to be called 'The New Criticism.' "

There is a distinct and specific biographical link. In the early and mid-1920s, Laura Riding, then living in New York, was an honorary member of the Nashville Fugitives at that time, while John Crowe Ransom was corresponding regularly with Graves about poetry and poetics. (The story of the visit of Riding to Nashville in December 1924 is among the more piquant episodes in southern letters; as Ransom wrote to Allen Tate somewhat later, she "did not realize that we had already established our respective personal relationships on satisfactory and rather final bases, and that we were open to literary relationships but not to personal.") Riding did have an involvement with—as might be guessed—Tate, who at one point was insisting that she and Hart Crane were the most important talents of the decade. It was Ransom who introduced Riding to Graves, who was taken with one of her poems, with momentous results. More important, of course, was the intellectual milieu in which these writers, who would soon develop in more formal fashion the method known as the New Criticism, existed. They absorbed Eliot's poetry and prose. They knew I. A. Richards's *Science and Poetry* and, later, *Practical Criticism.*

In *The Sun Also Rises* Hemingway has Jake Barnes and Bill Gorton discourse upon the fashionable employment of "irony and pity" in then-current critical parlance. As noted earlier, the use of ironic discourse goes considerably further back in time than the events on the Marne and the Somme; in First Samuel the women of Israel are reported as remarking to Saul: "Saul hath slain his thousands, / And David his ten thousands." But there can be little question that the chasm between civilized ideal and human actuality that the impact of the Great War laid bare shocked the literary imagination into a suspicion of abstraction and a preoccupation with what was tangible and concrete in language. Hemingway's oft-cited remarks in *A Farewell to Arms* about words such as "glory, honor, courage and hallow" appearing "obscene beside the concrete names of villages, the numbers of roads, the names of villages, the numbers of regiments and the dates" are to the point.

The New Criticism's penchant for irony and paradox was, after all, no more or less than an insistence upon protecting the language of poetry from tenuous, gauzy affirmations and vague claims to unearned significance, to safeguard the right of the poetic imagination to be taken seriously. The New Critics insisted that what was being asserted be carefully *looked* at; they wanted the poem to count for something, to matter: they wanted the reader to be given the opportunity to take part in the transaction, and not merely be manipulated by verbal and rhetorical sleight-of-hand.

Thus the instructional classic of the movement, *Understanding Poetry*, defines "irony" in the glossary to the 1950 edition in these words: "An ironical statement indicates a meaning contrary to the one it professes to give. . . "; and Brooks and Warren go on to remark that "irony, along with understatement, (in which there is a discrepancy, great or small, between what is *actually* said and what *might* be said), is a device of Indirect Method. . . . That is, the poet does not present his meaning abstractly or explicitly, but depends on the reader's capacity to develop implications imaginatively." Paradox was "a statement which seems on the surface contradictory, but which involves an element of truth."

The implicit relationship between such doctrine and the experience of 1914–1918 can be seen in a comment made in the introduction to *Understanding Poetry*, in which Brooks and Warren, in warning against the manipulation of human emotions through unexamined verbal associations, depose as follows: "Advertising, of course, raises the question in an extreme form. Advertisers naturally are not content to rest on a statement of fact, whether such a statement is verifiable or not. They will attempt to associate the attitude toward a certain product with an attitude toward beautiful women, little children, or grey-haired mothers; they will appeal to snobbishness, vanity, *patriotism, religion, and morality* [italics mine]."

In the same way, the insistence upon the primacy of the actual poetic text, and the importance of anchoring one's consideration of the poem in the language of the text itself, is surely the response to a cultural experience in which the public rhetoric employed to interpret what was happening on the western front, and the visceral, physical, and mental ordeal of human beings inhabiting trenches, produced an appalling discrepancy of meaning. The New Criticism was, in this sense, an effort to rectify the damage insofar as reading poetry was involved.

To return to the larger issue, I recall it being remarked, with some regret, when well into World War II, that unlike the Great War, there were no good American popular songs being written and sung about the event—no "Pack Up Your Troubles," "Keep the Home Fires Burning," "Over There," not even a "Mademoiselle from Armentières" or "You're In the Army Now." The virtuosi of Tin Pan Alley were grinding out the pop tunes, but it was without exception wretched stuff. Certainly there were obvious reasons—the lack of novelty about the experience, a larger public sophistication, the awareness this time of what we were in for, and so on.

What it came down to, however, was the fact that, in having to do what it was doing, the generation that engaged in World War II didn't see a great deal to sing happy or inspiring songs about. Generally it made do with the old ones, or else chose songs that had nothing to do with war and fighting. And that, it strikes me, was all in all a good thing. Clearly it had nothing to do with morale, civilian or military, which from Pearl Harbor through V-J Day was resolute. But it showed that while engaging in a war might be necessary (as indeed the defeat of Nazi and Imperial Japanese militarism was), there was nothing romantic or ennobling about doing so, but principally a distressing business of killing and surviving. Heroism there could be, and was, but it was heroism on the job, not on a football field or in the lists at Ashby de la Zouch. One can only hope that what these wars taught will continue to be remembered when all the actual participants in them have disappeared, and that our literature will allow us to forget neither the hideousness nor, even despite the frustrations of Ypres, the Somme, or, in World War II, Anzio Beach, the bitter necessity.

(1992)

'The Weasel's Twist,
The Weasel's Tooth':
The First World War as History

My favorite book in my very early teens was Floyd Gibbons' *The Red Knight of Germany,* a biography of Baron Manfred von Richthofen, who shot down eighty Allied airplanes before his own turn came. That the Red Baron had been a loyal servant of the German Kaiser, that Adolf Hitler was now flexing his military muscles for another go at it, that the Nazis were burning synagogues and arresting Jews, and that had I been a German instead of an American I and all my family would have been prime candidates for enrollment in a concentration camp, did not matter. If I thought about the contradiction in allegiance, it would have been to the effect that a high-principled Prussian nobleman like Richthofen would never have condoned the Nazis or flown planes in Herman Goering's Luftwaffe—which was patent nonsense. Such, however, was the logic of the young about such things.

I had already begun reading all the books I could find about the First World War, beginning at age nine or ten with an affair entitled *Army Boys in French Trenches.* There was also a novel for boys involving some youthful British sailors aboard a gunboat or destroyer named something like the *Sylph,* and climaxing, I think, with the sinking of the German commerce raider *Emden* by the Australian cruiser *Sydney.* By comparison with those, my discovery of Floyd Gibbons's biography of Richthofen represented a step forward in sophistication and authenticity; after all, it was non-fiction, and it quoted from actual documents and reports.

Needless to say, the depiction of that conflict in such books differed sharply from that in the works of literature I began reading in college and thereafter. Offhand I can't recall a single important novel or poem about 1914–1918 that deals with it as anything other than a bloodbath, which indeed it was. Its violent impact upon British writers, both as it was taking place and later, has been sorted out and interpreted authoritatively by Samuel L. Hynes in *A War Imagined: The First World War and English Culture* (1990). Before that, Paul Fussell, in *The Great War and Modern Memory* (1975), developed a largely convincing thesis that the trauma of World War I had imprinted fundamental patterns upon the way we thought and viewed our experience.

My concern here, however, is not with the effects, psychological or aesthetic, of the First World War on literature, but with the way the war has been presented as military history. For every book that has been published about 1914–1918, there have probably been five on World War II—which doesn't mean that there were not thousands on the earlier war. Between Armistice Day in 1918 and the Nazi invasion of Poland in 1939, barely two decades elapsed, and once the Second World War came along, few general readers wanted to read about its predecessor, so that not many new works of other than a scholarly nature were published on the 1914–1918 fracas. With a few notable exceptions this has continued to be true.

There are understandable reasons for it. In the first place, nothing was really settled by all the carnage of World War I; the outbreak of World War II two decades later was not so much the start of a new war as a recommencement of the previous one. True, the First World War caused, or in any event hastened, the breakdown of Tsarist Russia and the advent of the Soviet Union, and it brought an end to the Austro-Hungarian Empire. But the central issue of the fighting in 1939 when the Germans invaded Poland and Britain and France declared war remained the same as it had been in 1914: whether or not Germany was to rule Europe and become the dominant power in the Western world. Not until 1944–1945 was the question settled and were the German armed forces defeated on German soil and made to surrender unconditionally.

So a work of history that set out to interpret the First World War could offer its reader no real conclusion other than a chronological one, and to that extent it was deficient in dramatic resolution— a beginning, a middle, but no end. In effect, it was the non-fiction equivalent of a "slice of life" novel—more accurately perhaps, slice of death. Moreover, the individual military episodes had a sodden sameness about them. Unlike the Second World War, which was largely a war of movement, the War of 1914–1918 was mainly one in which the principal antagonists stayed in place for four years and butted heads together. In the fast-developing campaigns of World War II decisiveness, strategic imagination, and innovative leadership were important to what happened. On the Western Front in 1914–1918 this wasn't so.

Consider, for example, the fascination with the aerial aces of World War I, which exists even today. Only the other evening I watched a television documentary on the Red Baron. In the 1920s and 1930s youths like myself could reel off the names of, and the number of enemy planes downed by, Richthofen, Bishop, Ball, Fonck, Boelcke, Voss, Guynemer, Nungesser, and—the best we could do because of our country's brief involvement—Eddie Rickenbacker. We built balsa models of S.P.A.D., Nieuport, Sopwith, Albatros, and Fokker fighter planes. This was because fighting between aircraft was almost the only kind of combat in 1914–1918 in which what individual human beings did could be singled out, and particular warriors identified as heroes. Who were the commanders in charge of the various components of the offense and defense at Passchendaele, the Somme, Verdun? Does it matter?

By contrast, the leading army commanders in World War II were recognizable personalities. The campaigns they directed were distinguishable from one another, their outcome attributable in important respects to the quality of leadership. Not even on the Eastern Front was the strategy basically no more than that of attrition. This was true at sea as well; unlike Jutland in 1916, the naval battles of Coral Sea, Midway, and Leyte Gulf in the Pacific in 1941–1945 were decisive. Nor was there any difficulty in identifying the villains, for unlike what took place in the summer when the Archduke died, neither Germany nor Japan stumbled into war. On the contrary, they deliberately began it, were ruthless in their treatment of conquered territory and conquered peoples, and there could be no question about whether the rest of the civilized world would be better or worse off if the Axis Powers were to win.

For these reasons and others, then, the conduct of World War I has not been exactly a flourishing topic either for sustained historical analysis or for popular recapitulation. The best books about it have tended to be those which have sought to show how and why the war was allowed to happen. They make for melancholy reading, describing as they do the coming of a calamity that nobody wanted to happen, that could and should have been arrested, and that brought an end to an era in which the overall well-being of the citizenry of Western Europe was probably at a higher level than ever before in history. Each time we read it, no matter how familiar the events chronicled, there is the sense of helplessness and futility, the instinctive hope and wish that long-since-happened history somehow won't happen. Henry James's famous comment to Howard Sturgis after war came was and is to the point: "The plunge of civilization into this abyss of blood and darkness by the wanton fear of those two infamous autocrats is a thing that so gives away the long age during which we have supposed the world to be, with whatever abatement, gradually bettering, that to have to take it all now for what the treacherous years were all the while really making for and meaning is too tragic for any words."

Assuredly those in command—and also those who patriotically accepted their leadership—had no idea of just how dreadful modern warfare could be. What the high command in Germany and Austria-Hungary—along with some of the military leadership in Russia, France, Great Britain and Italy—did want, and expected, was something brief and exciting, along the lines of the Franco-Prussian War. Another literary reference, this time from Yeats's "Nineteen Hundred and Nineteen," is appropriate:

> Parliament and king
> Thought that unless a little powder burned
> The trumpeters might burst with trumpeting
> And yet it lack all glory; and perchance
> The guardsmen's drowsy charges would not prance.

The result was the hideous trench warfare of the Western Front, which Yeats's poem aptly characterized:

> We, who seven years ago
> Talked of honour and of truth,
> Shriek with pleasure if we show
> The weasel's twist, the weasel's tooth.

As for what happened to the human beings who made up the various armies once the fighting began, and who after a few months' time found themselves engaged in a warfare of attrition that was as monstrous and impersonal as it was unexpected, books of military history on the First World War have tended to be of two kinds. There have been military studies, which chronicle and analyze the events of the war in terms of the strategy and tactics used, and which are written by professional military historians, usually with military training. There have been more general works that concentrate upon showing just how terrible and futile was the mass slaughter of a conflict in which modern weaponry had rendered traditional methods of attack and breakthrough obsolete, yet the generals in charge seemed to know nothing better than to keep trying to use them.

While I do not claim to have read all the overall histories, I am familiar with a good many of them, and it seems to me that by and large this division still holds true. It is with this in mind that I want to comment upon on a new, and I think very good book, *The First World War: A Complete History* (1995), by Martin Gilbert.

Gilbert, who is well known for the multi-volumed biography of Winston Churchill—he took over after Randolph Churchill died and wrote six of the eight volumes, has centered his story on the officers and men in the ranks, describing what happened to numerous individual soldiers during the course of the various battles and campaigns. He states his intentions very clearly, and in his closing two sentences reiterates what he has been after: "All wars end up being reduced to statistics, strategies, debates about their origins and results. These debates about war are important, but not more important than the human story of those who fought in them."

To illustrate what this approach means for Gilbert's book, let me cite an example. For the first day of the Battle of the Somme, July 1, 1916, we are given three-and-a-half pages of narrative, taking up the following items, in the order cited:

1. A song sung by British troops as they moved into position.

2. A poem written by a 23-year-old participant in anticipation of the attack.

3. The preparatory artillery barrage.

4. The bulky, heavy equipment toted by the attackers, and two comments on its cumbersomeness.

5. The heroic action of a Scotch drummer in beating the charge and rallying the troops.

6. A lance corporal's description of men being mowed down by machine gun fire.

7. German machine guns in action, and their lethalness.

8. A passage from a lieutenant's letter home, telling of the Germans he had killed, describing how Germans fired upon his men until about to be overrun and then attempted to surrender, how most of them were not allowed to do so but were killed, how some Germans had allowed British soldiers to dress their wounds and then shot them in the back: "They are swine—take it from me—I saw these things happen with my own eyes."

9. Another lieutenant's description of a German soldier surrendering and begging for mercy—and apparently receiving it.

10. A medical officer's description of a man suffering from shell-shock.

11. A lieutenant's successful efforts to get his men to follow him over the top, his leading them into No-Man's Land, his being hit, being unable to keep going, taking refuge in a shellhole, crawling back to the British trenches and en route seeing "the hand of a man who'd been killed only that morning beginning to turn green and yellow. That made me pretty sick and I put on a spurt."

12. The capture of two German-held villages, and the figures on British casualties during the first day's fighting—more than 21,000 killed, and 25,000 seriously wounded.

13. The killing of 159 men by a single German machine gun, their burial in a trench, and the notice put over their grave: "The Devonshires held this trench. The Devonshires hold it still." Among them was the lieutenant whose poem was quoted earlier.

14. What happened to another battalion, 520 of whose 836 men were killed and 316 wounded, with lines from an unfinished poem by one of the dead, and what an official historian later wrote of the action.

15. A sergeant who was hit and went back for medical help, returned to the front line to rescue a soldier unable to make it back on his own, and was thereafter never again seen. This is followed by seven lines of a poem he had written entitled "A Soldier's Funeral."

16. The sergeant's brother's description of the dying and wounded at a dressing station.

17. A Newfoundland battalion that was almost totally wiped out, and a quotation from a divisional commander praising their valor.

18. The loss of more than 500 attackers taken prisoner, and the failure of the assault to reach an objective located less than ten miles from the starting point.

In closing, we learn that the British attack did force the Germans to give up trying to capture Verdun from the French, and also that a French attack that same day, though making larger gains than the British, failed of its objective but took 3,000 prisoners and captured 80 German artillery pieces.

The handling of the first day of the Somme is representative of Gilbert's approach throughout. Particularly for the Western Front fighting, almost every important campaign is similarly depicted, though not usually at such length. Certainly no one can complain that in his treatment of the opening of the Somme offensive, Gilbert has not given ample attention to the "human story of those who fought" in that battle of eighty summers ago.

It is interesting to compare Gilbert's version of what was happening with that in another good but very different one-volume history of about the same length, *The Great War, 1914–1918* (1959), by Cyril Falls, a British military historian who fought in World War I. Falls devotes less than a page to the actual fighting, concentrating on the preparation and the results. One of his announced objectives in writing his book was to refute the myth, as he calls it, that "the military art stood still in the greatest war up to date," and that its commanding generals were unimaginative elders who knew nothing better than to send masses of men over the top to get slaughtered.

Falls makes no criticism of Douglas Haig at the Somme, saying only that the British commander "must have been terribly disappointed that night" following the first day's fighting, but that "he was not yet aware of the terrible total of his losses." Later he declares that, no longer expecting a breakthrough then and there, "Haig had gone over to *la guerre d'usure,* the warfare of attrition," and: "So it went on, Haig imperturbable and nursing the hope that by mid-September the German resistance would be so reduced that a powerful assault might lead to a break-through."

Martin Gilbert's quite different view of Haig would appear to reflect his experience in writing the biography of Winston Churchill. He shares Churchill's distrust of the military leadership and abhorrence of its willingness to expend lives in fruitless Western Front offensives. Gilbert quotes Churchill's comment about the high command in a letter to an officer friend at the end of 1917: "Thank God our offensives are at an end. Let them traipse across the crater fields. Let them rejoice in the occasional capture of placeless names and sterile ridges." In Gilbert's book, Haig comes across as a military mandarin who throughout the war kept insisting that the German army was on the brink of collapse and who ordered offensive after offensive, each time trading huge casualty lists for what proved to be insignificant gains. The date of Haig's accession to command of the British Expeditionary Force in place of Sir John French, December 19, 1915, which was also the day when the Germans first employed phosgene gas against the British, is characterized by Gilbert as "an ominous day for millions."

The point is that Gilbert's approach to World War I, written by a man who is not a military historian as such, is concerned above all with showing its hideousness, its frightful human cost, its pathos and loss, and its essential failure to achieve its objectives. Because of that failure it was necessary to fight a Second World War, and if it hadn't been for the subject of Gilbert's biography, England might well have failed to stop Hitler. As prime minister during World War

II, Churchill was frequently at odds with his military leaders, and during World War I, as First Lord of the Admiralty and later in other capacities, he also tangled with the military professionals. "Do you think," he asked, writing to his wife from the Front in April of 1916, "we should succeed in an offensive, if the Germans cannot do it at Verdun with all their skill and science? Our army is not the same as theirs; and of course their staff is quite intact and taught by successful experiment. Our staff only represents the brain power of our poor peacetime army—with which hardly any really able men would go. We are children at the game compared to them."

Because in important respects Gilbert sees the events of both world wars through Churchill's eyes, this in turn puts him at odds with various military historians, many of them professionally trained soldiers and sailors, who have tended to depict Churchill as an interfering amateur in his dealings with the military, even while readily granting his essential role as wartime leader of his embattled nation in 1939–1945. Among such historians, Gilbert's reputation as a commentator on military affairs is not very high.

A certain amount of snobbery, I am afraid, is at work here, something not exactly unheard of in British social and academic circles. In addition to being a civilian all the way, with his military experience confined to two years of National Service in 1955–1957, Gilbert is a third-generation English Jew of Polish descent. The condescension and resentment with which some English "Establishment" military historians and their disciples have responded to Gilbert's work seems at times to reflect an attitude that he has no right to be writing about such things at all. (I confess that in reading *The First World War* I did have the feeling that he was overly zealous to demonstrate Jewish involvement in the war. If so, one can understand why this might be.)

In any event, and for whatever reason, Martin Gilbert's history of the First World War is concerned most of all to illustrate the enormous slaughter and wastefulness that were the product of a time in which, to quote Yeats again,

> Mere anarchy is loosed upon the world,
> The blood-dimmed tide is loosed, and everywhere
> The ceremony of innocence is drowned . . .

Using the skills of the research historian he has combed through wartime letters, diaries, memoirs, accounts of various kinds, seeking to demonstrate the reactions of rank-and-file soldiers to the fighting. Repeatedly he quotes from the poems written by men who are killed in action. The technique throughout is as much that of montage as sequential narrative, with the attention focussed upon those who did the fighting, not on those who planned it.

In effect, Gilbert's narrative method replicates the author's attitude toward the war on the Western Front as a thing of largely shapeless horror. A brief summation of the overall military situation at the time of a battle or campaign and a few sentences about what those in command hoped to accomplish are followed by a description of the carnage, with numerous illustrative quotations, and at the close a report on casualties. What comes across is not the military strategy or tactics, but the killing and suffering. As presented, there is a sameness to the successive battlefield ordeals, so that often it becomes difficult to distinguish what went on at the Somme from what took place at Ypres, Loos, Artois, Champagne, Verdun, Vimy Ridge, Passchendaele, Cambrai, the Aisne, etc., other than by casualty figures and proper names—which is precisely Gilbert's point. The tactics employed, the methods of attack and defense, the deployment of the troops involved are largely the same from one battle to the next, just as in almost every instance the results are equally indecisive.

By contrast, a professional military historian such as Cyril Falls goes at the war from a standpoint of the overall strategies employed and how they worked out, with emphasis upon how the military commanders on each side sought to win the war, and how and why they succeeded or failed. Each battle and campaign is depicted as a distinct and recognizable phase in a four-year struggle to defeat the enemy. In *The Great War, 1914–1918*, Falls by no means omits errors and failures; but he sees and depicts the war's military leaders as dedicated professional soldiers confronting an awesome responsibility and doing their best to win the war with the resources available to them. The result is that Falls's book provides a great deal more information about the conduct of military and naval operations and the performances of commanders and commanded.

One can understand that as a professional soldier, a participant in the war, and for sixteen years the official British historian of it, Falls would be loth to depict it as an incredibly botched affair, even though bravely fought. His summation of the ordeal and slaughter of the Somme, for example, is as follows: "Only high hearts, splendid courage, and the enormous endurance of the flower of the nations of the British Empire could have won the results attained. Only wonderful powers of resistance by the Germans could have limited them to what they were."

But what Falls's approach cannot do well is to convey the nature of World War I as what it so agonizingly was for those who fought it: a human disaster, a mass slaughter made only the more dreadful by the knowledge that it accomplished so little. Martin Gilbert's summation for the same campaign, by contrast, reads this way: "After four-and-a-half months of struggle, suffering and advance there was no concluding victory, or even coda: one divisional history recorded that two companies which had taken part in the assault on November 18 had disappeared 'entirely, being overwhelmed by machine-gun fire'."

For Gilbert, the central fact about the Somme is that despite the horrendous bloodletting of July 1, the attack was renewed the next day, and throughout the subsequent summer and autumn a steady stream of young men continued to be sent over the top to face the rifles, machine-guns, and artillery of modern warfare, in a battle of attrition that traded 420,000 British and 204,000 French casualties for 680,000 Germans killed and wounded—in order to take a strip of blasted earth less than ten miles deep at its very broadest, and scarcely twenty-five miles long.

There is something terribly chilling about Cyril Falls's comment about the end of the first day on the Somme, quoted earlier: "Haig must have been bitterly disappointed that night . . . " No doubt the general was indeed disappointed, but, coming as the observation does following a recounting of the first day's British casualties, the reader may be pardoned for thinking that other things besides Douglas Haig's disappointment might be remarked of the general who had just finished setting a new record, for the English-speaking world in any event, in single-day battle deaths for troops under his command. Whatever else may be advanced in criticism of Gilbert's *The First World War: A Complete History,* it cannot be said that he fails to get across to the reader the fearful butcher's bill for the War of 1914–1918.

Yet if we wish to understand the strategies and tactics of the Western Front, it is to books such as Cyril Falls's that we must turn. To concentrate on the horror is not enough.

Military history, if it is to do other than titillate the young and provide chairborne warriors with vicarious combat excitement, must seek to make as much sense as possible of battles and war. Showing the hideousness of it all will not suffice. At the same time, books about war that neglect to keep the reader continually reminded that what is being described is not a chess game, but that human beings are being maimed and killed by other human beings, can scarcely be said to have made proper sense of the subject, either. To concentrate on the problems of command while neglecting those of the commanded is no way to write about warfare, if the object is to make the experience of war understandable. Yet in the writings about the Western Front, these seem to be the alternatives.

It strikes me, in contradiction of the American title of Sir Philip Gibbs's influential memoir of 1920, *Now It Can Be Told,* that even though almost eight decades have gone by since the Armistice, and almost all who took part in the war are dead, a truly definitive account of the First World War has not yet been rendered—or if it has, then certainly I have not read it. The books about the war itself, as distinguished from the circumstances of its advent, continue to fall into two categories, those which effectively describe, interpret, and analyze the strategy and tactics, and those which concentrate on conveying the bloodshed and the horror. Thus for all its considerable merits, Martin Gilbert's book cannot be said to be what its subtitle claims: *The First World War: A Complete History.* It is graphic, it is evocative, but it is certainly not "complete." (To cite an obvious example, no attempt is made to show what that first day on the Somme might have looked like from the German side of No-Man's Land.) The "complete" history—by which I mean not in its details so much as in its perspective on the war—remains unwritten. We do not yet have an account of the First World War that does justice to the military history while also thoroughly recounting the shock and trauma of trench warfare on the Western Front.

It seems likely that to get such a book, or series of books, we will have to wait for at least as long as it proved necessary to do for a definitive history of the American Civil War—which is to say, until someone approaching the task with literary skill and historical rigor comparable to Shelby Foote's can manage the perspective and insight needed to master the subject. Ninety-three years had elapsed after the surrender of the last Confederate army before the first book of Foote's three-volume *The Civil War: A Narrative* appeared in 1958.

It was not merely happenstance, I think, that the first volume of Shelby Foote's *The Civil War* was published four years after the

Brown v. *Board of Education* decision was handed down by the U.S. Supreme Court. The Court's desegregation decision and Foote's Civil War trilogy were equally products of the *Zeitgeist*—to use a term drawn from a time when Germany was noted for its savants and artists rather than for less civilized kinds of activity. The intellectual and emotional climate was finally at a stage at which intellectual judgments could be sustained without diluting the author's sympathy for the human beings caught in the historical trap. There could be military history without the suspension of the knowledge of good and evil.

When will that be possible for the War of 1914–1918? Not for a long while, one suspects. In Martin Gilbert's *The First World War* there is a photograph of the battlefield of third Ypres, September 1917. The earth is a torn morass of mud and clods, stretching to the uneven horizon. The half-buried corpse of a soldier is sprawled in the foreground, appearing, in the black-and-white photograph, almost as if it were part of the terrain. Earlier in the book another photograph shows the people of Munich welcoming the coming of war in 1914. Around one of the throng of faces in the crowd is a circle, and an enlarged inset reveals an enthusiastic young Adolf Hitler.

(1995)

The National Letters

Babe Ruth's Ghost

Employing sportswriters to ghostwrite books by ballplayers is a custom that goes back into the dark abysm of professional baseball history. The need to do so is obvious. Patrons of the game are eager to read about how their heroes play it, and who better to tell of that than the hero himself? Yet almost by definition most professional athletes are unskilled at literary composition; the words *literary athlete* are, if not an oxymoron, then by all odds an unlikely combination, preposterous on the order of a taciturn disc jockey or a self-effacing U.S. senator. Someone else who is gifted at manipulating words rather than throwing or hitting a baseball must therefore come to the rescue—i.e., a professional sports journalist who is reasonably familiar with the working principles and personalities of the National Game.

The genre, to be sure, is not confined·to books about athletes. Military heroes are frequently in need of literary aid; for every U. S. Grant, who wrote his own memoirs, there have been dozens of illustrious generals and admirals for whom the pen was more cumbrous than the sword, and who sought help from less martially renowned but verbally fluent aides-de-camp. Politicians, industrialists—these too have employed ghostly assistance. But with ballplayers it is practically mandatory—the time in the limelight is so brief, the financial opportunity so obvious.

The roles of athlete and professional wordsmith in such a joint literary endeavor can range from fairly extensive collaboration over a period of months, with much interaction, to no more than a session or two with a cassette tape-recorder, in which case the ghost-writer will depend largely on record books and newspaper files for his material, and consult the athlete mainly to corroborate an occasional reference.

I read somewhere of a telephone conversation between Willie Mays, a gifted athlete, but not notable for his literary interests, and Charles Einstein, who assisted Willie in writing his memoirs, which reportedly went along these lines:

"Hello, Willie? This is Charlie."

"Charlie who?"

"Charlie Einstein. You know, the one who wrote the book."

"What book?"

Whether it actually happened I cannot say. The point is that, depending upon the concerned parties, the actual role of athletes in the research and writing of books of which they are nominal authors can be slight indeed.

The degree of involvement may also, though not necessarily, be reflected in the manner in which the collaboration is described on the title page of the book. The book in question can be written "by A *and* B," or "by A *with* B," or "by A *as told to* B," depending upon the wishes of the participants and the rectitude of the book's publisher. Or it can even be listed as having been written "by" A alone, with the fact of B's collaboration nowhere displayed.

I have to say that the standards for volunteering such information have improved in recent years. Rare is the ghostwritten sports book today that omits all mention on the title page of the presence of a professional collaborator in its preparation. In this respect the promulgation of such books is considerably more honest and straightforward than in the instance of ghostwritten books by celebrities in other fields of human endeavor, as witness the recent row between Lee Iacocca and the writer hired to ghost his best-selling memoir, or the books "by" numerous aspirants to high political office.

Mainly this is because, unlike politicians, business executives, generals of the U.S. Army and the like, most professional athletes feel in no way degraded by public knowledge that a literary work appearing under their names was not in fact written by them. In the circles they frequent, no disgrace is attached to such an arrangement. To repeat, it is nothing new: the practice has been going on for generations. To cite an example: *Pitching in a Pinch* by Christy Mathewson, which was published in 1912 and which remains one of the better baseball books, was penned not by the renowned Big Six of the old Giants but by John Wheeler, founder of North American Newspaper Alliance. This fact appears nowhere in the original edition and was revealed only in 1977, when the late Red Smith prepared an introduction for a new printing (*Pitching in a Pinch: or, Baseball from the Inside* by Christy Mathewson, with a foreword by John N. Wheeler, edited by Vic Ziegel and Neil Offen. New York: Stein and Day).

Nor did Mathewson have other than a nominal relationship to the juvenile novels issued under his name during the years of his pitching renown. It is doubtful that he even read the latter until they appeared in printed form, though he may have checked the baseball material to see that no obvious improbabilities were included. I suspect, however, that *Pitching in a Pinch* does contain considerable information that was actually furnished by Mathewson himself.

In the 1920s the ghostwritten sports book entered upon its full splendor. The audience for sports underwent a vast expansion during the Prohibition decade, and the demand for "as told to" books intensified accordingly. It was not the custom then, however, to let it be known to the public that literary assistance may have been given to the athlete-author in the writing. As with Mathewson's book of

the previous decade, such books were normally presented as having been penned solely by the sports hero whose name was cited on
the jacket and title page.

I recently came upon a gem of the ghostwriting genre: *Babe Ruth's
Own Book of Baseball* by George Herman Ruth. The Babe, of course,
was the supreme sports figure of his era; his renown surpassed that
of all other Americans, even including movie stars and U.S. presi-
dents. A book written by him could be counted upon to sell numerous copies, and in 1928, the year in which his book appeared and
which immediately followed the season in which he hit sixty major
league home runs, this was true in spades.

As was and is well known, the Bambino was no litterateur. He
possessed only a reform-school education, and as a reader it is doubtful that he ever during his lifetime willingly sweated his way through
the contents of an entire book, much less composed one himself.

To assist him with his literary endeavors, G. P. Putnam's Sons
secured the services of a ghostwriter, who, as Jerome Holtzman notes
in his introduction to the University of Nebraska Press's Bison Books
reprint edition (1991), was the late Ford C. Frick. At the time a sports-
writer for the New York *Journal*, Frick later became president of the
National League and then commissioner of baseball. During the
1920s the Christy Walsh Syndicate frequently employed him to assist
the Babe to cover the World Series and other baseball doings.

The late Fred Leib offered a revealing story in his book *Baseball
As I Have Known It* (1977). On one occasion Ruth and several of his
Yankee teammates, while traveling aboard a Pullman car, were discussing his collaborator, who had been working with him for several years. The Babe, Lieb wrote, called over to him: "What's the
name of the guy who writes for me? It rhymes with 'quick,' 'thick,'
'Dick.'"

"The name is Frick," Lieb told him. "Ford Frick."

Exactly how the Ruth-Frick collaboration worked is not recorded,
but it is possible to make certain assumptions, based upon the pub-

lished text itself as well as upon all that we know of the Babe's way of doing things. Here, for example, is a passage in Ruth's book, appearing in a chapter entitled "Batters and Batteries," during which he takes as his exemplars several performers on the New York Giants of the era previous to that in which Ruth played for the Yankees:

> So far as a pitcher is concerned, good catching means everything to him and poor catching means his ruination. That's true even of veteran pitchers. No matter how much natural stuff a pitcher may have he can't pitch well unless he has absolute confidence in his catcher. And certain pitchers and catchers work together so long that the pitcher is lost pitching to any other man. Mathewson and Myers were such a team. Matty always pitched to Myers and despite the fact that Bresnahan was a great catcher, he and Matty never were able to team up successfully. Roger on the other hand could handle Bugs Raymond like a whiz, while Myers was lost with Bugs' pitching.

Now there are several things wrong with Ruth's published discourse as processed through Frick. In the first place, the tenures of Roger Bresnahan and Chief Meyers—Frick spelled the name incorrectly— on the Giants did not overlap. Bresnahan left the club after the 1908 season, whereas Meyers, although joining the Giants late in 1908, got into no games until the 1909 season. Moreover, when Bresnahan departed, it was to go to St. Louis as catcher-manager, in the trade that brought Bugs Raymond to the Giants for the first time. So Raymond could not possibly have worked with Bresnahan. And as for Mathewson's alleged inability to pitch well when Bresnahan was his catcher, the latter was in place behind home plate for the Giants during each of the three World Series shutouts that Mathewson tossed against Philadelphia Athletics in 1905.

It was, however, apparently true that Meyers did have trouble working with Raymond, and vice versa. What probably happened was that Bresnahan's role was being confused with that of yet another Giant catcher of the era, Art Wilson, who is cited in Mathewson's book as having caught Raymond "almost perfectly."

Ruth's information on the history of major league pitcher-catcher relationships, therefore, was considerably skewed. Was it Ruth's information at all?

I doubt it. Very likely Frick, who knew Ruth's milieu well and had ghostwritten newspaper columns for him in the past, chatted with him a few times, took some notes (this was long before the day of the cassette recorder), and composed *Babe Ruth's Own Book of Baseball* pretty much by himself.

My guess is that when Frick interviewed Ruth on the topic of pitcher-catcher relationships—if indeed he ever actually did so—the conversation proceeded along something like the following lines:

FRICK: "How about the catcher, Babe? Is he important to the pitcher?"

RUTH: "Sure. Somebody's got to catch the [expletive deleted] ball."

FRICK: "Yes, but what I mean is, when you were a pitcher did it matter to you whether a particular catcher was behind the plate? Did you have one catcher that you preferred to throw to?"

RUTH: "Nah, just so they could catch the [expletive deleted] ball and throw through to second, I didn't give a [expletive deleted] about who was back there."

FRICK: "Still, some pitchers do have favorite catchers, don't they?"

RUTH: "Oh, I guess so. Maybe a few of them."

FRICK: "Somebody told me once that Matty—you know, Christy Mathewson, on the Giants—liked to pitch to Chief Meyers, but not to Roger Bresnahan."

RUTH: "Oh yeah?"

FRICK: "So I understand. On the other hand, they say that Bugs Raymond couldn't work with Meyers. He had to have Bresnahan."

RUTH: "Could be, I never seen either one of the [expletive deleted]s pitch, myself."

To all but the most uncritical of readers, the prose style of the book's opening sentence reveals quite clearly who will be doing most of the ensuing writing and thinking: "My earliest recollections center about the dirty, traffic-filled streets of Baltimore's river front." The pronoun is that of the Bambino, but the nouns and adjectives and verb are assuredly the voice of Ford Frick.

At times Frick did attempt to adapt his style to the Ruthian vernacular; "Old Jack Quinn of the Athletics is another man who has a delivery that's a pippin"; "And control! Say, that Collins had better control of his slow one than most fellows have of their fast ones"; etc. For the most part, however, Ruth's ghostwriter stuck to a more formal mode, and made little effort to make his prose mirror the Babe's way of talking—which, since Ruth is known to have used four-letter words reflexively and at all times, was just as well.

In ghostwriting the Babe's book Frick faced a daunting task. For from all accounts Ruth had little gift for recall and none whatever for reflection. He lived almost totally in the present, was largely unconcerned for anything but his own personal doings, took almost no interest in the lives and activities of his teammates except as affecting him, and was without awareness of or curiosity about the complexities of personality. The retelling of amusing anecdotes, the accumulation of colorful diamond lore—such was not his forte. For the most part he couldn't even remember the names of most of those who played with and against him; habitually he addressed each and all as "kid."

Ruth knew the game of baseball itself extremely well, but as a trade, in much the same way that a plumber can be master of the art of plumbing without having psychological insight into other pipefitters or thoughts about the décor of bathrooms, kitchens, and basements. The Babe could discourse on hitting, but not the mannerisms of individual hitters; he could describe the technique of the hook slide but convey little of the competitiveness and ferocity of those who utilized it well.

Frick was also up against the problem that Ruth was a public figure, a busy man; and there must have been a severe time limit within which the project had to be completed. Written with the impact of the fabulous 1927 Yankee season to give it vogue and topicality, it was designed to come out the next year. All Frick could do was to set his book's overall design, sketch out his chapters, set up a few sessions with the Babe, ask for explanations of techniques and procedures and seek to prompt comment on people and events, and then sit down at his typewriter and begin writing. As Jerome Holtzman notes in his introduction to the 1991 reprint, "From my experience as a ghostwriter, I know that eventually the writer must fly solo."

There are several passages in which Ruth is made to hold forth on the virtues of Tyrus Raymond Cobb, the Georgia Peach who dominated pre-Ruthian baseball. As might be expected, Cobb's skill at stealing bases evokes a lengthy tribute.

Now Cobb, who by inner nature and style of play came close to being an outright psychopath, detested Ruth and the long-ball game into which baseball had been transformed by Ruth's slugging prowess, and he took bitter umbrage over having been supplanted by the Babe as the game's chief luminary.

Ruth, by contrast, was not the hating type—he liked little kids, good-looking women, and almost everybody else. But that he had been stung by the Georgia Peach's often-voiced contempt for himself and what he exemplified, and quite justifiably resented the older player, is certain. On several occasions the two of them almost came to fisticuffs.

It seems, therefore, unlikely that, recognizing though he did the extraordinary skill with which Cobb hit and ran the bases, left to himself the Babe would have opted to devote several thousand words in praise of Cobb's intelligence, judgment, technique, and pluck. Ruth's discourse on base stealing even includes an anecdote, "one of the funniest lines I ever heard," in which a noted catcher of the early 1920s, Wally Schang, was asked by Connie Mack to tell what he would do if Detroit trailed by one run, Cobb was on second base, and Schang knew that he was about to steal. "I'd fake a throw to third then hold the ball and tag him as he slid into the plate," Schang replied.

It is possible that Ruth actually volunteered the anecdote, which was well known among players and sportswriters and had seen print before; but it is far more likely that Ford Frick had heard and remembered it, thought it appropriate to the matter under discussion, and inserted it in the book. In all probability the conversation that resulted in Ruth's lengthy eulogy of Ty Cobb's skills went something like this:

FRICK: "How about base runners, Babe? Who would you say was the best? Cobb?"

RUTH: "Yeah, I guess you'd have to give the [expletive deleted] credit."

From there Frick, in Jerome Holtzman's metaphor, flew solo. Yet it should be understood that Ruth would almost certainly have had no objections to Frick's extended tributes to Cobb's skill at playing the game. What appeared in a book, whether allegedy written by him or anyone else, was of small concern to him. That he even bothered to read the book he supposedly wrote seems dubious to me.

It is unfortunate that in writing the book Ford Frick did not check his facts, and so avoided "quoting" Ruth on historical impossibilities such as the Bresnahan-Meyers comment. Still, in 1927–1928 a baseball ghostwriter struggling to complete a book on a deadline did not have available to him such reference works as Reichler's *Baseball Encyclopedia,* Thorn's and Palmer's *Total Baseball,* Neft's and Cohen's *Sports Encyclopedia: Baseball,* or other compendia presenting the year-by-year performances of former players in readily accessible form. To check up on such matters Frick's sole recourse would have been to comb through the successive yearly volumes of the Spalding and Reach guidebooks; and if the book was to be ready for the 1928 season, there was little enough time to spare for research.

Besides, did it really matter very much? Then as now the principal audience for "as told to" sports books, whether labeled as such or not, consisted of teen-agers and young adults—but far less informed in sports history and versed in statistics than their present-day counter-parts. To be sure, doubtless there were certain knowledgeable New York fans—by Ruth's heyday they were coming to be called that, rather than "cranks" or "bugs" as in the earliest years of the century—who instantly recognized that Roger Bresnahan could not possibly have caught the games that Bugs Raymond pitched for John McGraw's Giants, and who remembered very well that he had been Mathewson's battery mate throughout the famous all-shutout World Series of 1905. But nobody expected Ruth to get his facts right anyway. What the Babe knew how to do was to hit a baseball, not write about doing so.

Today's "as told to" ghostwriter has it much rougher. In 1928 there was no Society for American Baseball Research in existence, with a militant multi-thousand membership dedicated to the accurate compilation and extrapolation of baseball data. Nor were the sportswriters of the so-called Golden Age of sport nearly so sophisticated, so alert to the history and minutiae of their professional subject matter as their counterparts are today. What could pass without comment or disapproval then would be swiftly spotted and castigated now.

More than that, the likelihood nowadays is that other ballplayers themselves, or a goodly number of them, would read the ghostwritten book, with a critical eye not only for personal innuendo but for professional accuracy and soundness. For reading—which Rogers Hornsby for one always took care not to do during the playing season, on the theory that his batting eye would be adversely affected (he made an exception for racing forms)—is by no means an unheard-of habit among today's major leaguers.

But reading is one thing, and writing quite another. Therefore the sports ghostwriter still actively plies his trade. The tendency in recent decades, in some quarters at least, is to imitate the ballplayer's mode of discourse with uncensored exactitude of idiom. Indeed, one suspects that to add piquancy and photo-realism to the presentation, the vernacular voice is even given intensification. Thus Peter Golenbeck as alter ego of Sparky Lyle in *The Bronx Zoo* (1979):

> After what Reggie [Jackson] did tonight, all the mustard in the world couldn't cover him. He hit a single to right, and as he rounded first, he gave one of his stares at [Lyman] Bostock in right as if to say, "Go ahead, challenge me, you motherfucker." Bang, Bostock fired the ball in and picked him off first base. Challenge me, my ass. It made me so sick because there is absolutely no reason for that. And what I thought was interesting was that nobody said a word. It used to be "Look at that crap." Everyone would bitch and moan to each other about it. Billy [Martin] would go crazy. Now everyone goes "Oh." Ellie [Hendricks] said, "Did you see that?" I said, "Yep," and that was all there was to it. I went back to the john and fed my black widow another moth.

This may have been Sparky Lyle's actual, cassette-recorded language. The conventions for reproducing the spoken word in books have been considerably liberalized since the Golden Age of sport in the 1920s. It was obviously of no concern to Dr. Lyle that his musings be presented in such fashion by his collaborator, and without any important recognition of a possible distinction between spoken and written language. Clearly Mr. Golenbeck and his publisher thought it literarily desirable to make the young adult readers of *The Bronx Zoo* believe that they were being given the authentic, unbowdlerized discourse of playing field and locker room. Yet, all things considered, I think I prefer Ford Frick.

(1993)

The Passionate Poet and
the Use of Criticism

Like styles of interior decoration and ways of cutting the hair, poetic fashions change. What Thomas Stearns Eliot thought and wrote in the late 1940s and early 1950s, when as a young reader and would-be writer I was making his acquaintance, was considered almost canonical in its authority. Nowadays, as a critic he is out—way, way out. This is scarcely an occasion for surprise, because no author could maintain the kind of hegemony that Eliot did for very long; otherwise literature and literary taste would have to stand unchanged in their tracks.

Purely as poetry, nobody has succeeded in dropping "The Love Song of J. Alfred Prufrock," "The Waste Land," "Gerontion," etc., from the body of poetry in the English language that is to be read and absorbed. Harold Bloom can go on and on about the anxiety of influence, and claim that Eliot was overrated, that "the academy, or clerisy, needed him as their defense against their own anxieties of uselessness," and so on, but to any fair-minded observer it must be obvious that the imprint of Eliot's way of writing verse remains upon every serious practitioner of the art.

It is Eliot's critical personality, not his poetry or even his poetical personality, that is being repudiated. He was a poet who also wrote a great deal of criticism, which in its day was also highly influential, both for what it said and because of who was saying it. The criticism carried social, religious, and political ramifications, and not only the poetics but the politics of literature were involved.

More than any other critic Eliot was responsible for the intensified interest in the English Metaphysical poets during the 1910s, 1920s, and thereafter. He did not rediscover them; for one thing, they had never been completely lost, and during the nineteenth century good poets on both sides of the Atlantic read and valued them, even if popular anthologists, such as Francis Palgrave in his widely read *Golden Treasury,* slighted them. It was Herbert J. C. Grierson's edition of the Metaphysicals, published in 1912, that occasioned Eliot's essays. Yet it seems safe to say that had not Eliot championed Donne, Marvell, Herbert, Cowley and their contemporaries so powerfully, and tied in their poetics (and to a degree their politics) with the poetry of modernism that he and others were engaged in writing, so that a vote for Donne was a vote for modern poetry, so to speak, rather less would have been heard about the Metaphysicals during succeeding decades. As it was, to assert an interest in the Metaphysicals was to assert one's freedom from literary Victorianism.

The public face that Eliot showed in his criticism and—or so it seemed at the time—his poetry was that of the antiromantic, the severe moralist who would suppress the brazen assertion of personality through immersion in the literary tradition. He introduced the term "dissociation of sensibility" to describe what he saw as a chasm between thought and emotion that has afflicted the Western world at least from the late seventeenth century onward. His own fondness for the seventeenth-century Metaphysical poets lay in what he considered their ability to fuse the material and the spiritual world within the tropes of an imagery that invested physical objects with emotional significance.

In retrospect, however, there seems to have been notably less suppression of personality on Eliot's part than everyone thought; what we took as reticence was more along the lines of impassioned self-mortification. Indeed, it is difficult to think of a poet of any era the rhythms of whose verses throb with more autobiographical passion than Eliot's, while his criticism, which once seemed so calm and magisterial, now appears to constitute a strenuous and even desperate insistence upon personal coherence in the face of near-chaotic emotions.

II

The cultural and historical situation out of which Eliot emerged was similar to that of elders and contemporaries such as Henry Adams, James Russell Lowell, John Jay Chapman, Owen Wister, and other scions of the older, pre–Civil War American upper-middle class which felt itself in danger of being supplanted by newly rich vulgarians. The Eliots were Boston and Cambridge all the way, even though the poet's grandfather, a distinguished Unitarian educator and theologian, had gone out to St. Louis, Missouri, in the 1830s and founded Washington University and the St. Louis Academy of Science.

It was axiomatic that Eliot, with his literary inclinations, would be educated at Harvard. What was not axiomatic, however, was that he would proceed to turn his back on the fashionable culture of Cambridge and Boston, and the high-minded, rational theology of New England Unitarianism, with its creed of moral uprightness and public service. For all that, however, he shared with his social peers a sense of being deprived of a privileged role by the leveling impact of industrialized urban democracy.

Eliot arrived in England in the summer of 1914 when the imminence of war caused him to cut short his doctoral study in Germany. His intention was to return to Harvard, defend his dissertation, and join the philosophy faculty there. Previously he had tried Paris, but found it tawdry and vulgar. England, however, was the proper place for him, and it did not take long for him to realize it. For Eliot was a *snob*—who was also a great poet. Among the qualities he liked about England was that its class distinctions were visible, open, and need not be blurred by egalitarian theory; subordination was built into its way of doing things.

He did not become an Anglican until the mid-1920s, but the spiritual crisis that led him to High Church orthodoxy dated from the early 1910s. The poems that placed him at the head of modernism were written not from a standpoint of belief, but the compulsive appetite for it, by a man who very much feared he might be damned to Hell (and who was also greatly drawn to the role of martyr). A considerable amount of arrogance is necessary, of course, to be able to view oneself in terms either of martyrdom or eternal damnation, but Eliot had no trouble managing it.

The technique he developed, mostly on his own, to write his verse was precisely what the poetry of his time required—intellectual rigor, concrete imagery, allusive reference, complexity in general. He and his generation were still very much in revolt against the high Victorians, whose example hung on. The Edwardians had proposed little more than a relaxation in the formal use of adjectives and nouns, whereas what was required was considerably more drastic—the overthrow of a pervasive cultural ideality that used high-sounding abstractions to minimize contradiction, and that avoided the historical duality of mind and matter through sentimental transcendence. Poetry, if it is to mean anything beyond inspirational utterance, must offer immanence; but the late Victorian, *fin de siècle* poetry could manage only a kind of wistful regret at the inability to escape the toils of mortality.

In the hands of the great Victorians, poetry in English had been able to address itself to a very large, educated audience, but the price paid for that kind of mass communication had turned out to be too high by far, because once the immediate excitement wore off, the poets had begun to write not merely *to* but *for* that audience and had developed a language convention and a set of ornamental emblems to facilitate the process. By adopting a specialized poetic diction, the poetry of waning Victorianism denied poets the right to document their own everyday experience. In subject matter, attitude, and vocabulary, the dominant verse of the late nineteenth century was tailored to what a cultural consensus of educated English and American middle-class taste and opinion was willing to approve, and as always happens, the absence of controversy soon produced a listless apathy.

What Eliot and his generation set about doing was to restore importance and intensity to poetic utterance by breaking up the cultural consensus. The modernists, as they came to be known, wanted no comfortable across-the-board agreement between poet and expectant audience, for the price of such agreement was intellectual platitude and emotional pablum. Eliot's enthusiasm for the English Metaphysicals was in part simply that, as Samuel Johnson had declared, they forced the reader of poetry to *think.* "We can only say that it appears likely that poets in our civilization, as it appears at present, must be *difficult* . . . ," Eliot wrote in 1921. "The poet must become more and more comprehensive, more allusive, more indirect, in order to force, to dislocate if necessary, language into his meaning."

The impact of the First World War had the effect of greatly reinforcing this attitude, because the chasm that opened up between the rhetoric of patriotic nationalism, on the one hand, and the horrendous, impersonal lethality of trench warfare on the Western Front, on the other, called into question the poetic abstractions and slogans through which the values of Western civilization had been articulated.

The footnotes that accompanied publication of Eliot's "The Waste Land" in 1922, in addition to commenting on the text of the poem, had a specific rhetorical function to perform. *This Poem Is Difficult,* they announced to an audience that was in effect being told to choose between intellectual complexity or blandness. *If you want to read the poem, you had better not be put off by the threat of having to use your intelligence, because this poem is not going to do your thinking for you in advance.*

Eliot in later years minimized the role of the footnotes, declaring them a spoof and saying that he wrote them to help fill out the pages of a too-thin volume. And doubtless the element of spoof was involved, but it was an insiders' joke, meant for the amusement of the initiated—which is to say, for the audience for modern poetry, which was a severely reduced audience by comparison with that of the poetry it had supplanted.

What Eliot did in his early poetry was to get down to the here and now. J. Alfred Prufrock himself may have been wistful and longed for transcendence; but the poem offered a flesh-and-blood character about whose physical immersion in the world there could be no doubt. Prufrock might say things fuzzily; the poem describing him as he did so was concrete. It was, moreover, psychologically complex: whenever Prufrock essayed a pose, he was quick to recognize and identify it *as* a pose. He was neither naïve nor vain; and he was *intelligent.* And because he was, intelligence was required to understand his situation.

III

There was, however, considerably more to Eliot's aesthetic than the advocacy of verbal complexity, intellectual rigor, and linguistic precision in poetic utterance. His preference for the Metaphysical poets and the Elizabethan and Jacobean dramatists carried cultural ramifications. He was deliberately reaching back to a language convention that antedated John Milton as well as the Romantic and Victorian poets (of the eighteenth-century poets he had little to say, because it was no part of his aesthetic to find merit in a poetry based upon rhymed couplets and personification). In so doing he was rejecting a poetics that involved the open assertion of individual personality, in favor of a more stylized utterance. One doesn't find Elizabethan poets writing sonnets about their own blindness, or their career frustrations at the age of twenty-two. In terms of their personal experience we scarcely know *who* the Elizabethan poets were. The key to Eliot's critical stance, I think, lies in just that: an abhorrence—one might even say a terror—of the unabashed declaration of personal identity on the part of a writer.

Significantly Eliot tended at all times to skirt the presence of Shakespeare, because even though the same kind of anonymity characterized Shakespeare's verse, the sheer richness and inimitability of the language was such that it called attention to itself and, by implication, the author composing it. Eliot's attack on *Hamlet* is famous; he based it upon what he considered was the assertion of the poet's personality in excess of the logic and plausibility of the protagonist's characterization, insisting that the secret of Hamlet's dilemma lay outside the play and in its author's personal consciousness. It was on this occasion that he coined (or reinvented) the term "objective correlative," declaring that the writer must find an objective—i.e., anonymous—image or symbol for his personal emotion, and that Shakespeare had failed to do so. This was nonsense, for a writer can— as Milton, Wordsworth, Keats and others did (including, as we shall see, Eliot himself)—assert his own personality in such strong and unmistakable terms that his emotion assumes palpable and believable form. The true sticking-point was that the distraught Prince of Denmark was in personality too close to a Romantic poet—i.e., to a person of acute sensibility, sicklied o'er with the pale cast of thought—for Eliot to feel comfortable in his presence.

Eliot disapproved of *all* the Romantics and Victorians, even Arnold, because not only did their aesthetic call for the outright assertion of personal sensibility, but also the sensibilities being asserted were for the most part not to his liking. One might think, for example, that a poem such as Arnold's "The Buried Life" would have appealed powerfully to Eliot:

But often, in the world's most crowded streets,
But often, in the din of strife,
There rises an unspeakable desire
After the knowledge of our buried life;
A thirst to spend our fire and restless force,
In tracking out our true, original course. . . .

But even that was too public, too communal: "*our* buried life," "*our* true, original course"—and besides, the poem goes on to say that when "a beloved hand is laid in ours" and "Our eyes can in another's eyes read clear," then "what we mean, we say, and what we would, we know. . . . " Prufrock, by contrast, realizes that "It is impossible to say just what I mean!" and that even if one could do so, there was every likelihood that it would be neither understood nor accepted. In short, Arnold's civilized melancholy would not do; what Eliot wanted expressed was civilized desperation.

His desperation. Yet one mustn't express one's own private desperation. *That* was the problem. What Eliot wanted to do, and he constructed a poetics that would enable him to do it, was to achieve a naked, unqualified expression of social, intellectual, religious, and sexual desperation—while appearing not to be personally involved at all! The truth is that Eliot was himself a dyed-in-the-wool romantic (how could he not have been given his time and place?), but his own assertiveness took the form of an intensely self-conscious rejection of overtly public emotional assertion.

He called this "classicism," linked it to monarchism and Anglo-Catholicism, and announced it as his program. Yet however its outward form may have resembled classicism in the 1920s and 1930s, when it was in full flowering, it was in motivation and psychological stance at the furthest remove from any kind of classical severity, sobriety, and proportion. As we now realize from Eliot's published correspondence and Lyndall Gordon's two excellent biographical volumes, for Eliot his poetry was a way of asserting an intensely personal appetite for suffering, an agonizing fear of sexual appetite, and a shrinking from carnality, along with a desperate need for religious certainty and for civic and social coherence.

Here was no mere disgruntled Henry Adams, concerned over loss of supposed ancestral privilege and lamenting the erosion of government by the Best People; this was a man in full emotional recoil from democracy, the middle class, religious latitudinarianism, and the cramp of the flesh. His adopted English identity became a badge of virtue to signify his emancipation from vulgarity. Following his conversion, he used High Church Christianity as a weapon to defend himself against the excesses of political and social democracy, and also as an antidote to lustfulness.

Reading the edition of his letters from childhood through the year 1922, edited by Valerie Eliot, one is struck by the extent to which this man shared emotionally and intellectually in almost none of the political and social assumptions that we assume are characteristic of the ideological heirs of Thomas Jefferson and Abraham Lincoln. He used the word "European" to contrast with "American," and saw the latter as threatening the civilized integrity of the former (this was before the Second World War, of course). He was, all in all, a man thoroughly and desperately in flight from his country, his origins, his family, the academic career the family had expected of him, and from his own carnal appetite. And he shaped a series of antithetical responses into a poetics, an aesthetic, and, indeed, a theology and politics.

IV

"Poetry is not a turning loose of emotion," Eliot wrote in a famous essay, "but an escape from emotion, it is not the expression of personality, but an escape from personality. But, of course, only those who have personality and emotions know what it means to want to escape from these things" ("Tradition and the Individual Talent").

My point is that T. S. Eliot was a powerful personality, and that personality *is* powerfully expressed, not escaped from, in his poetry and criticism. "The Waste-Land" and "Gerontion" may *look* like the "objective correlative" he insisted that the poet's emotions must assume and that Shakespeare supposedly failed to exhibit in *Hamlet*, but only because it is in the form of negation. That is, because especially in his earlier poems (and, indeed, at least until *Four Quartets*) Eliot chose to depict his own contemporary society predominantly in terms of images drawn from his frustration, revulsion, disgust, and sense of loss, and he identified what he portrayed as *not himself, not his own*. In that sense they are "objective"—but far from being "an escape from personality" they constitute, in their "not me," a passionate assertion *of* that personality.

In his old age, Eliot admitted as much, declaring that "The Waste-Land" was no more than the expression of a private peeve against the world. As it indeed was, but it was so powerfully expressed that it answered both the poetic and the emotional needs of a considerable audience. Otherwise it could never have had the vogue and influence it enjoyed.

He was greatly talented, and intensely ambitious. Poets who have programs and agendas cannot wait on their poetry to secure them a hearing and further their careers. They write criticism, make friends with editors. With calculated skill, Eliot set about the conquest of literary London. Consider the implications of the following, written in 1919 in the course of a letter explaining why he has turned down an editorial position offered him by the *Athenaeum*:

> There is a small and select public which regards me as the best living critic, as well as the best living poet, in England. . . . I really think that I have far more *influence* on English letters than any other American has ever had, unless it be Henry James, I know a great many people, but there are many more who would like to know me, and I can remain isolated and detached.

> All this sounds very conceited, but I am sure it is true, and as there is no outsider from whom you would hear it, and America really knows very little of what goes on in London, I must say it myself.

He is writing to his mother, and is concerned to justify his choice of a literary rather than an academic career, and moreover is aware that his parents in St. Louis probably believe he has squandered his talents and is wasting his life. Still, the terms in which he describes his success seem so thoroughly predicated upon reputation, and his satisfaction at his reputation thus far so obvious. The view he takes of what he has accomplished shows a highly realistic, even brazen acknowledgment of what it is that he has been seeking in literary London. It cannot be gainsaid that he found it.

Eliot's literary criticism is filled with the articulation of his own emotional needs and assertions. He was a master at giving the appearance of disinterested objectivity, while in fact pursuing his own calculated goals. He used criticism, as he freely admitted in later life, to advance the kind of poetry he was writing, and he was none too gentle in how he went about denigrating whatever did not contribute toward that objective. His famous rejection of Milton's poetry in 1936 is an example. To watch him in action as he advanced toward his goal with, shall we say, waffled oars is to view a master at the art.

His opening sentence is a classic. "While it must be admitted that Milton is a very great poet indeed, it is something of a puzzle to decide in what his greatness consists." It *must* be admitted—an onerous chore, you understand, something that one doesn't wish to do or enjoy doing. Did his audience share the reluctance? It seems highly unlikely—but putting the matter as he does, Eliot averts his audience's anger, because, after all, he *is* saying that Milton is a great poet. Still, great in what way? The pretense is that justifying one's praise of the poetry of John Milton is going to be a difficult business.

Second sentence: "On analysis, the marks against him appear both more numerous and more significant than the marks to his credit."

It *is* going to be hard to do, he concedes, but, so help him, somehow he is going to try to find a way to commend John Milton's poetry. "As a man, he is antipathetic. Either from the moralist's point of view, or from the theologian's point of view, or from the psychologist's point of view, or from that of the political philosopher, or judging by the ordinary standards of likeableness in human beings, Milton is unsatisfactory."

Unsatisfactory to whom? Why, to the speaker, of course; but since the speaker is obviously the very image and embodiment of Fair Play and reason, then maybe there *is* something wrong with a poet we had always thought of as being an ornament to English letters.

What is really unsatisfactory to the speaker, of course, is that Milton was a Puritan, and a regicide, and a supporter of Oliver Cromwell, and in favor of a republic rather than a monarchy, and above all the inventor and wielder of a style so formidable and expressive that the powerful personality of the poet infuses every line of his work. And all that *is* unsatisfactory and offensive *if* one is by contrast an Anglican and a believer in social subordination and a convert from the inherited political philosophy of Thomas Jefferson and Abraham Lincoln to the adopted political philosophy of Sir Robert Filmer and George III—and *also* the wielder of a formidable, inimitable personal style.

To resume the scrutiny of what John Hayward labeled as "Milton I," Eliot goes on to say that Milton subjected the English language to deterioration, and though a great literary artist was a bad literary influence. I cannot refrain from quoting in full one paragraph of quintessentially Eliotic demolition:

> There is a large class of persons, including some who appear in print as critics, who regard any censure upon a 'great' poet as a breach of the peace, as an act of wanton iconoclasm, or even hoodlumism. The kind of derogatory criticism that I have to make upon Milton is not intended for such persons, who cannot understand that it is more

important, in some vital respects, to be a *good* poet than to be a *great* poet; and of what I have to say I consider that the only jury of judgement is that of the ablest poetical practitioners of my time. ("A Note on the Verse of John Milton")

As I read that paragraph, it first declares that anyone who will not let the author flail away at Milton without protesting is stupid. The first clause of sentence two then makes a distinction between "good" and "great" poets that appears to imply that routine competence is better than poetic genius, and that this is "important." Again, important to whom? The second clause of the sentence informs the audience that no one is permitted to have an opinion on the subject except other poets, and only the very best of these. Yeats? Pound? Auden? Who else, in 1936? Surely not Robert Frost!

Taken all in all, the paragraph is Eliot at his best, a classic of aggressive assertion, written on the theory that in literary skirmishing, offensiveness is the best possible defense. (James Joyce could have done no better.) He goes on to say that Milton had no visual imagination, that his language is ("if one may use the term without disparagement"!) "*artificial* and *conventional*," and that instead of a fusion there is a division between sense and sound in his poetry. He compares *Paradise Lost* to Joyce's *Finnegans Wake* (at the time still known as *Work in Progress*), sees both as blind alleys for the literature, and concludes that Milton has "done damage to the English language from which it has not wholly recovered."

This was not the end of it, of course. In "Milton II" (as Hayward calls it), a lecture to the British Academy in 1947, Eliot takes it all back, or rather, he says that he meant what he said at the time, but only *for* the time. The reason is that what his own generation of poets was engaged in doing back in the 1920s and 1930s was getting the language of poetry back into contact with everyday vernacular speech, extending the range of its subject matter to cover modern experience, and getting rid of the idea that poetry should be restricted only to certain kinds of material. To achieve this, "the study of Milton could be of no help; it was only a hindrance."

The revolution had now (1947) been accomplished, however. The language of poetry was sufficiently up-to-date, and it was time to go on to other things, such as seeing what kinds of variations and developments could be managed within the now-accepted language, and also keeping it from becoming *too* up-to-date, *too* addicted to the vernacular, and so on. Since Milton was, outside of the theatre (i.e., Shakespeare), "the greatest master in our language of freedom within form," it was all right to admire him again: "In short, it now seems to me that poets are sufficiently removed from Milton, and sufficiently liberated from his reputation, to approach the study of his work without danger, and with profit to their poetry and to the English language." *At last he rose, and twitched his mantle blue; / Tomorrow to fresh woods and pastures new.*

Now in 1947, when Eliot announced that Milton was on the approved list again, he had published *Four Quartets* four years earlier, and he was more or less done with lyric poetry. (He was finished with some other things, too, including an insane wife who had made his life close to a hell on earth until he left her in 1933, and then had continued to harass and embarrass him until she was confined to an institution in 1938. In 1947 she died,). In the 1930s he had written two verse plays. Now he turned full time to the drama, producing three comedies which were highly successful on the commercial stage. For writing verse plays, Milton constituted neither model nor menace; the language convention appropriate to drama was at opposite ends from that for lyric poetry. For, that is, *T. S. Eliot's* lyric poetry.

The plain truth is that in terms of the poetic personalities manifested through their verse, John Milton and T. S. Eliot have more in common, are more alike, than almost any other two major poets in the English language. Allowing for differences in historical idiom, as poets they think alike, they sound alike. There is the same moralizing sensibility, the same habit of delivering sonorous *ex cathedra* judgments. This is not usually realized. Listen, however, to their alternating voices, their personalities as makers of lines and words:

> The place of solitude where three dreams cross
> Between blue rocks
> But when the voices shaken from the yew-tree drift away
> Let the other yew be shaken and reply

> As killing as the canker to the rose,
> Or taint-worm to the weanling flocks that graze
> Or frost to flow'rs, that their gay wardrobe wear

> . . . .

> In vials of ivory and coloured glass
> Unstoppered, lurked her strange synthetic perfumes,
> Unguent, powdered, or liquid—troubled, confused
> And drowned the sense in odours. . . .

> With all her bravery on, and tackle trim,
> Sails filled, and streamers waving,
> Courted by all the winds that hold them play,
> An amber scene of odorous perfume
> Her harbinger, a damsel train behind?

> . . . .

> O dark dark dark. They all go into the dark. . . .

> O dark, dark, dark, amid the blaze of noon. . . .

> . . . .

> I said to my soul, be still, and wait without hope
> For hope would be hope for the wrong thing;
>   wait without hope
> For hope would be love of the wrong thing. . . .

"Thoughts, whither have ye led me? with what sweet
Compulsion thus transported to forget
What hither brought us? hate, not love, nor hope
Of Paradise for hell, hope here to taste
Of pleasure, but all pleasure to destroy,
Save what is in destroying: other joy
To me is lost. . . . "

These poetic personalities are not so much antithetical and contradictory voices, as they are *rival operators*. Who else, except perhaps William Wordsworth, could use the high style so satisfactorily, combine Latinate and Anglo-Saxon diction so variously and flexibly? *Who else could through cadenced and intensified language assert a powerful personality quite so unmistakably?* The fact that the one was a Puritan and the other a High Church Anglican is unimportant; both wished to place the muse of poetry in the service of theological truth, and clearly each was also privately seeking to convince himself that it was indeed *truth*.

The theological positions, as noted, made them competitors; the poetry they wrote, and their attitude toward it and toward the politics of poetry and poets, made them rivals, and Eliot responded to it without a moment's hesitation. In Milton's day one did not write critical prose to manipulate the audience and undercut the competition, or assuredly the author of "Lycidas" would have written it:

Fame is the spur that the clear spirit doth raise
(That last infirmity of noble mind)
To scorn delights, and live laborious days. . . .

In Eliot's day it was done, and he went about it with a masterful assiduity.

As noted, there has been a powerful critical reaction against Eliot's position. He expected it, and would not have been surprised, though perhaps its vehemence might have dismayed him (*he* had been savage with his elders in his own day, but in his later years he grew quite benign.) The revolt has been mainly along political rather than poetic grounds. His role has been attacked as snobbish (which it was), antidemocratic (which it also was), and cold-blooded and intellectual (which it decidedly was not.) His way of voicing the assumptions of Anglo-Catholicism, so popular in the 1940s and 1950s, comes across as terribly provincial and restricted in a world in which Christianity is very much a minority faith, and High Church Anglicans only a tiny, if socially elite, segment of that minority. It would be difficult for all but a small remnant of properly sanctified readers to view the theological situation precisely as Eliot sketched it in 1931:

> The World is trying the experiment of attempting to form a civilized but non-Christian mentality. The experiment will fail; but we must be very patient in awaiting its collapse; meanwhile redeeming the time; so that the Faith may be preserved alive through the dark ages before us; to renew and rebuild civilization, and save the World from suicide.

It is essential, however, to keep in mind that Eliot was doing the greater part of his writing about Christian societies and the like *before* the implications of that particular kind of cultural and social exclusivity were made manifest.

Eliot's hard-won High Church style has been used by some of his more superficial admirers to justify a kind of smug superiority to the common herd of middle-class citizens striving to cope with the necessities of earning a living and paying taxes. The desperate struggle for belief, the craving for order amid chaos, the hard-won accommodation of soul and body that characterized Eliot's own tortured religious experience—these can be neatly bypassed by a bloodless, self-centered, privileged sanctimoniousness that holds itself aloof from the modern world and chastises godless materialism even while sipping Bloody Marys and driving Volvos.

On the political, as well as the social and theological front, Eliot's position *was* vulnerable, and remains so. And on the literary front, there seems little reason to go along with his contention that not only Milton but Blake, Wordsworth, Coleridge, Shelley, Byron, Keats, Tennyson, Arnold, Browning, as well as Whitman, Dickinson, etc., represent a falling off from the supposedly healthy, predissociated literary sensibility of the sixteenth and early seventeenth centuries. This is a bit much, as they say.

Yet do his detractors come off any better? I must say that what the revolt against Eliot and what he stood for and advocated, as conducted by Harold Bloom, Geoffrey Hartman, and others of the so-called "Yale School" (now largely dispersed), would substitute in its place seems pretty shoddy stuff to me. As between the "dissociation of sensibility" on the one hand, and the use of the word "elitist" to stigmatize anyone who finds Shelley's "Indian Serenade" vacuous, it becomes a matter of "Go it, bear; go it, dame." The idea that the ultimate dramatic satisfaction lies in "a High Mass well performed" seems no more specious to me than (to quote Bloom) "The mind of Emerson is the mind of America, for worse and for glory. . . . " If so, then God help us.

More importantly, almost all of that sort of thing is in Eliot's criticism, not his poetry. And when we look at the body of his literary criticism, what seems obvious is that not only was it usually placed in the service of his poetical ambitions, as he admitted, but also that most of it—including all the essays that attracted so much attention in the 1920s and 1930s—remains of importance principally because it was written *by him.* We can read it with pleasure because we can watch him at work defending his turf and cutting down the competition. He was a master contestant, no doubt of that. An American in flight from his cultural and social situation, he set out to establish himself at the top of the British literary cosmos, and he succeeded. As Allen Tate wrote to Donald Davidson from London in 1928, "There is something very American about Eliot's whole procedure, and I like it. He came here unknown and without influence. In fifteen years he has become the acknowledged literary dictator of London. What I like is that he doesn't seem to feel the role." (Tate was wrong, however, about the last.)

But it is the *poetry* that matters, and that lasts. It survives the man, and it justifies him *as* a man because it testifies to and embodies the agony. "Poetry is not a turning loose of emotion, but an escape from emotion"—so asserted one of the most passionate, desperate men ever to write verse. His poetry is *not* an escape from passion; it is not *about* the passion. It *is* the passion, for it is the poet, the personality, who is speaking the lines and uttering the language. "The Love Song of J. Alfred Prufrock" is placed in the mind of a middle-aged gentleman who hears the mermaids singing but not to him; but what gives this early poem its power is the communicated sense of frustration, the struggle between decorum and libido, the contempt for mannered response juxtaposed with the dread of vulgarity. "The Waste-Land" is no diagnosis of contemporary society from outside and above; it is the articulated and agonized depiction of a participant sharing in the chaos, and the organization by juxtaposed montage is part of the condition of fragmentation. And so on.

These things are *in* the poetry, *are* the poetry. The notion that the cold-blooded poetic craftsman is drawing upon the man's human emotions to provide an "objective correlative" in language and symbol is not so much false as simply inaccurate, when expressed in such terms. The passion is present, for the poet and the reader alike, *in* the disciplining as well as the outpouring, and is communicated through and within the naming and versifying.

From the earliest lyrics through "Little Gidding," the poetry throbs with the communicated emotion of a powerful personality, who is not least in evidence when he affects to be unconcerned. We cannot read a stanza of Eliot's poetry without sensing at once that we are in the presence of a passionate man, who moves words, image clusters, and stanzas around with calculated bravado, and knows all the tricks of the trade:

> That was a way of putting it—not very satisfactory:
> A periphrastic study in a worn-out poetical fashion,
> Leaving one still with the intolerable wrestle
> With words and meanings. The poetry does not matter.

It *does* matter; it matters so much that to save it from being undercut by irony he will pretend here that it doesn't—*in* a poem. Because if there is one thing that is more true of Thomas Stearns Eliot than of almost any other poet of his century, it is that neither in his verse nor in his life could he separate his personality into tidy, discrete segments. The voice is of a whole, a unified organism. But *not* one of harmony, balance, moderation—rather, a unique arena, a single sentient consciousness, made up of thought, emotion, desire, loathing, frustration, beauty, achievement.

How to account for his influence? In part for the reasons I noted earlier, about the condition of the art of poetry in the early decades of the twentieth century. In part merely because, as he himself said, young men who think they know the answers and act upon that assurance attract attention (as for example a braggart like Robert Bly, who had *nothing* to say about the art of poetry but gained an audience for a time through sheer bravado and loud-mouthed assertiveness). But mainly Eliot was influential because he was not only a superb poet who got all of his personality into his poetry, but a poet whose verse strategies, whose *technique,* offered a model for shaping a response to the experience of his time and place. He showed his contemporaries *a way to express passion in language.*

In his public and his social life he could offer the illusion of having so compartmentalized his experience so that he could be now this, now that—poet, critic, publisher, Anglican layperson, humorist, philosopher, pornographer (or scatologist rather), ascetic, and so on. But the poetry gave the lie to the appearance. Walt Whitman's line, "I was the man, I suffered, I was there," is an apt epitaph for this poet who thought his American predecessor a vulgarian and poseur (and who baldly coopted Whitman's hermit thrush for his own use).

Eliot's complete poems, 1909–1950, are a virtuoso performance of monumental proportions. In their revelatory honesty and their ability to cast the most recalcitrant and refractory material into language and so convert it into art, they yield priority to no other verse of their time—not even Yeats'. To my mind they exhibit, through what they show of their author, so much of what makes poets the barbed, difficult creatures most of the good ones are (*Here we go round the prickly pear*).

In his life, his dealing with others, he wrote and did some wretched, lamentable things. For all his first wife's repellant qualities—and from all accounts, including her own in her letters, she must have been an absolute demon on wheels—it is clear that in marrying T. S. Eliot she had come up against an ego that could not unbend or forgive. There was no way that marriage could have worked, because neither party was then in a position to identify or accommodate the other's dimly articulated needs. He was up against a virago; she was up against a male version of Charybdis. He could not help it; indeed, having contracted the engagement he assumed the burden manfully. Yet without "the awful daring of a moment's surrender" on his part there was no chance. And he could not manage it.

All this is in the poetry. The further away in time the historical figure recedes—if he were still alive he would be 103 as I write this—the more complete, and awesome, the poetry seems. Even today, during the full tide of the critical reaction against what he represented politically, socially, his verse cannot be ignored, and has not been. It is the day of the Harold Blooms: "Eliot is a poet whose poems, with some exceptions, tend to become weaker rather than stronger, the more provocatively they trope, defensively, against the burden of anteriority." (Come and trope it as you go, with a parricidal toe. Eliot asked for it, all right—and he got it. Bloom's whole protesting body of criticism is testimony to the *strength* of Eliot's influence.) But good poetry outlasts criticism and outlives fashion. We have no finer, more passionate poetry than Eliot's, and deserve no better.

(1992)

The Grand Panjandrum
of Wellfleet and Talcottville

Sometimes it is possible to know too much about an author.

The seriatim publication of the journals of Edmund Wilson, begun with a volume for the 1920s and culminating with that for the 1960s and early 1970s, has had the effect, for this reader at least, of considerably diminishing the stature of the man who kept them. When writing about himself instead of about other writers, he comes off mainly as tedious, humorless, and egotistic beyond all normal expectations.

When the volume entitled *The Twenties* appeared in 1975, the combination of naiveté and self-importance prompted me to write a parody. But the final installment, *The Sixties: The Last Journal, 1960–1972* (1993), touches off no such mirth; one's emotions range from passive boredom to active disgust, depending upon whether he is reciting the dreary particulars of social life in Talcottville, New York, or describing the details of those occasions when he engages in sexual intercourse with his wife.

There is also much trivia—it is almost *all* trivia, come to think of it—about partying, dining, gossiping, and general cultural-vulturing in New York City and Wellfleet, among such as Auden, Isaiah Berlin, Stephen Spender, Anita Loos, Arthur Schlesinger, Jr., Jason and Barbara Epstein, Dawn Powell, and so on. Surely these people can't all be as supercilious as depicted here.

It is a curious business. The question that constantly comes to mind is, Why, and for whom, was he writing all this? It is all very well to say that he was writing it for nobody else but himself, that he was setting down his experience in the way that a captain keeps a ship's log, which is to say, simply for the record. But that won't do; he worked it over, interpolated comments. Beyond doubt he expected it to be published some day.

Why, then, place on display nasty remarks about one's daughter's bouts with mental illness? Why tell about the sexual pliancy of a young woman assistant who presumably will still be married to her husband when the diary gets published? (Wilson had no way of knowing she would die at age 54.) What, in short, is gained by the gratuitous posthumous infliction of pain and embarrassment?

The only answer would seem to be that this man believed himself to be so important, and his life and work to be of such momentous artistic significance, that nothing that happens to him must be suppressed. *Amicus Plato, sed magis amica veritas.* (This is not consistently observed, of course; as we know, he sometimes suppresses experience unflattering to himself.) There is vanity enough at work here to make William Wordsworth or the late Leonard Bernstein seem like modest men by comparison.

To be sure, one may admire the artlessness of a man who describes his daily toilet habits on the Cape—each morning he seats himself on the throne and reads packets of reviews of his earlier books. (Most of the reviews, he complains, are poorly written.) But the assumption that humility and virtue exist in being ruthlessly revelatory about oneself doesn't hold up here. This isn't candor. It's self-infatuation, boasting. He thinks that by setting down the details of his experience he is creating a work of art!

So, apparently, does his editor; "Probing in its observation, uncomfortably familiar," Mr. Dabney writes, "*The Sixties* makes us all players on the stage of our daily lives, elevating the isolated individual struggle to the heroic." Well, perhaps—but damned if it seems very heroic to me. For I can't read it merely as a man's matter-of-fact observations about himself and his experience, the decrepitude of his body, the musings of his mind. The performance is too self-conscious; he is playing the role of ☞ EDMUND WILSON RECORDS HIS EXPERIENCE 🖙 . Perhaps it should be taken a step further—this is a watchbird watching a watchbird, etc.—and be thought of as a portrayal of honest self-conscious pomposity, but it won't work, for myself at least. The actor isn't up to the demands of the role.

I seem to be running down a literary genre, the journal, and certainly that would be foolish, for I can think of people who systematically kept diaries and journals that are both fascinating to read and extremely valuable for the portrayals of times, places, and people. The Duc de Saint-Simon is only one such; there are Boswell, Mary Boykin Chesnut, the Goncourts, Hester Thrale, Samuel Sewall, Pepys, and so on. What then is the difference? Why do Edmund Wilson's seem so fatuous?

One reason is that Wilson in the role of keeper of a journal can't tell me anything of real significance about the famous people he knows—not even Scott Fitzgerald. His literary and social gossip about Wellfleet in the summer is a forlorn business, largely because his casual view of people is superficial. He doesn't have much to provide in the way of intuition; one doesn't have the sense of any kind of Joycean epiphany being observed in action.

What Edmund Wilson has to offer as a writer isn't and never was spontaneity or sudden intuition. It is, rather, intelligent analysis—what he can make of something by thinking about it, the relationship he can perceive between a writer's biography, the history of the writer's time and place, and the literary work itself. After reading *The Sixties* I went back and reread a number of his books, beginning with *Axel's Castle* and including *To the Finland Station, The Triple Thinkers, The Wound and the Bow, Classics and Commercials, The Shores of Light, A Piece of My Mind, Patriotic Gore, The Bit Between My Teeth, The Dead Sea Scrolls,* and *The Twenties.*

I was struck with the contrast between Wilson as literary journalist and as personal recorder. There are times, to be sure, when the literary journalist is showing off—boasting of having read all of Alexander Stephens's *Constitutional View of the War Between the States*, of learning new languages so as to read books in the original, of translating some but not all of Verlaine for us, and so on. But Wilson's virtue as a commentator is the thoroughness and saneness with which he goes about the task of informing us about books. He performs, better than just about anyone else in his time and place, the function of the really good critical journalist—he shows us what's there, places it in context, interprets its significance. Compare him with, say, Malcolm Cowley, and you mark the greater range, the larger curiosity, the relative absence of bookishness. Compare him with H. L. Mencken (a better writer, a virtuoso of the language), and Wilson is so much the more informative reporter, and there is seldom a hidden agenda at work as with Mencken. As long as his subject is other than the everyday life and observations of Edmund Wilson, he is a pleasure to read.

Alfred Kazin, who in the third volume of his memoirs, *New York Jew*, offers several memorable depictions of Wilson, thought *Patriotic Gore*, subtitled *A Study in the Literature of the American Civil War*, his best book. A very good book it is, too, offering readings of numerous books having to do with the American Civil War. I can understand why Kazin would rate it so highly, for at the time it was published—1962—it offered much the most informative attempt as yet to set down what, intellectually and literarily, that conflict was all about from the standpoint of the participants. When I read it over this time I was impressed by just how much of it was paraphrase; there is page after page of plot summary, extensive recitation of the biographies of the authors and memoirists. This was by no means a weakness; Wilson was, in the best journalistic tradition, giving us the evidence. His way of making a point is always by piling up illustrative data. It was, however, sometimes a self-indulgent affair; I found myself skipping through the lengthy and quite unnecessary plot summaries of fiction by Albion Tourgeé, John W. DeForest, Harriet Beecher Stowe, and even George W. Cable (on whom, however, Wilson was quite informative.)

There is relatively little overt interpretation. The passing of judgment comes principally in the Introduction, written at a time when the Cold War was in full swing, and also when Wilson was in trouble with the I.R.S. for having failed to pay his income taxes. Wilson depicted the War To Save The Union as the act of a sea slug swallowing a smaller sea slug. Very properly this upset numerous reviewers. What struck me about it this time around was just how simplistic Wilson's analysis was. A good case can and should be made for the near-hypocrisy and self-deception inherent in the wartime slogans, and the far greater role of economic and political opportunism than the protagonists on both sides admitted. But Wilson didn't make that case. He scarcely even looked into it. He merely—in his Introduction, that is, not in his individual essays—wrote off the whole complex and genuinely tragic struggle as mere reflexive biological behaviorism. The contrast between the reductive Introduction and the subtlety and complexity of the books and people discussed was exasperating.

I have to say that there was a certain amount of arrogance to *Patriotic Gore*. Kazin didn't pick it up. But there was the authorial assumption, *passim*, that until he, Edmund Wilson, has looked into the subject of the American Civil War, it simply can't have been looked into properly. This was scarcely true. Since it was something that I had long been interested in myself, when I read it in 1962 I kept noting things that he should have known about but didn't, interpretations and explanations that he apparently didn't realize existed, discoveries he was making that had long since been discovered. In reviewing it then I didn't stress the point, for I felt that, considering the overall performance, it would have been ungrateful.

Rereading the book again (I have returned to it often over the decades) I found that I couldn't go along with Kazin's rating of *Patriotic Gore* as its author's best—not in the sense of most interesting. It is too much of a sampler, too random in its inclusions and exclusions. A fine book it is all in all, but one could do a pretty good job of understanding the Civil War literarily without it. The same certainly isn't true about the subject matter of *The Shores of Light* and *Classics and Commercials,* those two collections of his articles, review essays, and random writings of the 1920s, 1930s, 1940s, and 1950s. These are random pieces, not focussed in subject matter like those in *Patriotic Gore,* but one couldn't imagine trying to write intelligently about the American literary scene from the end of the Great War through the aftermath of World War II without constantly turning to what Wilson had to say. That was Wilson's true milieu. From the pages of the *New Republic* and later the *New Yorker* he offered his commentaries, and they are as much a part of the literary scene as Ring Lardner, the Algonquin Round Table, Charles Scribner's Sons, the critical authority (from London, via transatlantic liner) of T. S. Eliot, and the pervasive emanations of Marxist class consciousness from the canyons of Manhattan.

Wilson himself got a good infusion of Marxism early on, moving right into it from the Sacco and Vanzetti troubles, and there isn't a time from the late 1920s onward that it doesn't affect his thinking, whether positively or, later on, in the sense of reacting to it. With the Great Depression weighing everybody's imagination down for a half-dozen years or more, those writers who spent much time either living in or else reading and thinking about what was being set into type in New York City and the metropolitan Northeast had an extremely difficult time not being knocked off their pins by the Third International.

Wilson kept his head better than the Granville Hickses and John Chamberlains, was seldom crudely reductive, and like most intelligent literary folk was by the late 1930s drawing a distinction between the Marxist-Leninist brand of communism, as it was then known. and the Soviet-style dictatorship of Joseph Stalin and the Moscow-directed Party Line. But for years afterward, there was the implicit assumption in much of his social thinking that the revolutionary social vision of Lenin had been betrayed, which carried with it the corollary that true Marxism was a genuine, if untried, alternative to Western capitalism.

As he gradually relinquished his attachment to the Marxist ideal, he didn't replace it with a zeal for the wonders of business capitalism, however, as his friend John Dos Passos and so many other ex-Marxists did. Instead he retreated into a deep social pessimism; henceforth it was a matter of one sea slug vs. another.

His book *To the Finland Station,* however little read nowadays, is a formidable piece of work. An account of the intellectual origins of Marxism, the timing of its advent was singularly unpropitious—1940. The Nazi-Soviet pact had disillusioned all but the most dedicated Party members, Western Europe was in Hitler's grip, and it was clear that only the English stood between us and a world dominated by totalitarianism, so that we had better rush all available aid to them while rearming ourselves as fast as possible. It was no time for considering how communism got started.

Wilson began the book in the early 1930s, when Soviet communism appeared to many to be the solution to the seemingly uncontrollable self-destructiveness of finance capitalism. By the time it neared completion, things looked quite different. En route, therefore, Wilson was forced to shift his ground considerably, and to interpolate (one assumes) a lengthy explanation of why Marx didn't understand about the United States of America, couldn't credit the self-corrective possibilities in Western democracy, and understood the nature of the proletariat so poorly that he couldn't foresee the alliance of state socialism with nationalism that produced Nazism, fascism, and Stalinist communism. What Wilson wasn't really able to concede, however, was that there might be something fundamentally wrong with the view of human nature that underlay socialist theory. (When in the 1950s this conclusion became inescapable, he sank into the sodden, "a plague in both your houses" pessimism that characterized all his later thinking about society.) But *To the Finland Station* is a remarkable book. Nowhere else is there a more lucid and interesting portrayal of the socialist and Marxist thinkers, from Michelet through Marx, Engels, and Lenin. There are chapters on Renan, Taine, Anatole France, Babeuf, Saint-Simon, Fourier, Owen, Enfantin, Lassalle, Bakunin, and Trotsky. Wilson handles it as chronological narrative; mixing ideas, ideology, biography, history, and psychology. With his usual dogged thoroughness when undertaking a new project, he learned Russian and German in order to read what was written in the original. What Malcolm Cowley wrote in 1940 still goes: Wilson "has removed the communist fathers from the realm of dogma and carried them into his own world of letters; he has stripped them of the pedantries that covered them as thickly as Marx's whiskers and has revealed them as remarkable men who never ceased to be human beings . . . He has the novelist's gift for revealing personality in action, the dramatist's gift for bringing characters into conflict, the poet's gift for finding concrete symbols to express abstract ideas and complicated psychological states; and yet he does not give the impression of being specialized in any of these fields." It wasn't his fault that the wine was turning into vinegar even as he chronicled the vintage.

The volume of Wilson's which played the most creatively useful role of all his books—it has not, however, stood up best over the generations—was beyond question *Axel's Castle: A Study in the Imaginative Literature of 1870 to 1930*. Appearing in 1931, this one performed a momentous task: it told the intellectual reading public how to read and to think about the literature of modernism. Moving from the French symbolists through Yeats, Valéry, Eliot, Proust, Joyce, and Stein, Wilson did an excellent job of (in no invidious sense) popularizing those masterworks that through language and form opened up the complexities of twentieth-century sensibility to literary use. True, the theoretical context of the work has been marred by some crude Marxist sermonizing, no doubt interpolated as the Depression expanded, but as always with Wilson it is what he explicates, shows and summarizes about literary works, not what he decides they should mean, that matters. *The Wound and the Bow* (1941) continued the work, this time with Freudian psychoanalytical insights (likewise rather crudely applied).

These two works, so important and influential when they appeared, don't hold up particularly well in detail, for the reason that our critical perceptions of the authors and works he was writing about have long since been developed with considerably more subtlety by others. But it was Wilson who held open the door for the public to come inside and look around.

He wasn't, to be precise, a critic of notable subtlety and deftness, and this even though he did do so much to make the intellectual climate safe for Joyce, Proust, Eliot, etc. When one reads Wilson now on, say, Joyce, one realizes that he didn't always quite get the point. On the other hand, he was taking what was happening seriously, doing his best to illuminate what for most general intelligent readers were still opaque surfaces, not throwing up his hands and fulminating about obscurity, authorial capriciousness, four-letter words, and so on. One has to keep in mind always that he was writing critical journalism in a magazine and newspaper marketplace characterized by the limited tastes of such as Clifton Fadiman, Christopher Morley, Alexander Woollcott, Henry Seidel Canby, Bernard DeVoto, Edward Weeks, and—rock bottom—J. Donald Adams. As writers on literature for periodicals, none of these gentlemen possessed either Wilson's intelligence or his imagination. To use Van Wyck Brooks's fuzzy but handy terms, he was a highbrow who was writing critical journalism for an audience dominated by middlebrow critical intellects, and who was able, in the age of Sinclair Lewis, Joseph Hergesheimer, Michael Arlen, and Stephen Vincent Benét, to persuade no small number of readers to have a go at

Joyce, Proust, and Eliot.

Still, for Wilson, the fiction of his friend John Dos Passos, before he turned conservative, was the ultimate in what an American novelist ought to be doing. With certain exceptions—James Branch Cabell, for example—he preferred his writers to deal with the here-and-now. He didn't like excursions into metaphysics. Emerson *si,* Melville *no.* He liked Henry James, but was always a bit uneasy over the absence of action. At the same time he undervalued Samuel L. Clemens, failing to recognize how much subtlety lay within that seeming artlessness. Too much stylistic intricacy, too subtle a role for the narrator in what was being presented, and Wilson got into trouble.

William Faulkner he missed almost totally, and with Robert Frost he seems to have been quite unable to look beyond the pastoral surfaces. Wilson's sensibility was so totally urban, his imaginative horizons so completely restricted to cityscapes, that almost the only way he could read twentieth-century literature not set in cities or else rooted in class consciousness was as farce. This meant that this champion chronicler of the National Letters was unable to read either our greatest twentieth-century writer of fiction or one of our two foremost lyric poets (the other being Eliot.) Oh well, Sainte-Beuve was blind to Stendhal and Baudelaire.

For all that, Wilson's range was certainly quite catholic when compared with most. He mixed literature, history, lexicography, pop culture; he could write on Firbank, Stephen Potter, mushrooms, Houdini, Teddy Roosevelt, Kipling. When he became interested in the Dead Sea Scrolls he produced a book that told the general public more of what was involved than had hitherto been told or has been managed since. Not itself scholarly, his book earned the respect of the experts.

How, then, could the man write so well and usefully, and yet, when he turned inward rather than outward for his subject matter, show himself up so dismayingly? That, ladies and gentlemen, is the mystery to be unraveled; but alas, such things defy definitive solution, since all the biography and depth psychology in the world can't account for individual responses to external phenomena. Still, here is the precocious, prodigiously intelligent, overly mothered son of wealthy, prominent parents, brought up in protective seclusion in Red Bank, N.J.,—i.e., spoiled rotten. Then abruptly he is plunked down at the Hill School, to cope on his own. A teacher's pet, clearly he isn't at all good at what commands respect among his peers, which is to say, sports and sex. But then he gets to Princeton, where the ground rules change, physical prowess no longer rules the roost, and being a gentleman becomes the fashionable thing. Whereupon he turns dandy, comes into his own. joins the equivalent of the Princeton Junction lodge of the Swinburne Society, edits the *Nassau Lit*, dominates the artistic crowd (including the impressionable young Scott Fitzgerald), and from there moves naturally and inevitably up the line to Greenwich Village, where he is ready, as a certified young Ivy League intellectual and Future Leader of America, to help conduct the national letters. (The same was then being done in England, with, however, somewhat different results, for there the process was more institutionalized and secure.)

I exaggerate, to the point of caricature. Still, there is something comic about the performance—and also something very pathetic. Socially and emotionally he is so very much less developed than he is intellectually, and it is necessary then and always afterward to fake the common touch, hide behind his skill at words, play the role of savant. Fortunately Edna Millay arrives from Upstate and he is relieved of his virginity. (He wanted to marry her, but that particular candle was much too busy burning at both ends.) He comes into his own as critic; his range, his erudition astonish them all. He weds an actress, it doesn't work out; there is a lengthy affair with a lass of lowly caste but spritely *derrière;* he has a nervous breakdown; he marries again (there will be four wives in all before he is done), and so on. During much of this time he is going back to Red Bank on weekends; his now-widowed mother is raising his daughter by his first wife, and inevitably he makes a large point of complaining about the food and asking for more money.

The discrepancy between the public personality, the Brilliant And Creative Critical Journalist, on the one hand, and the thwarted lover and resentful, dependent son, on the other, papered over as it is by a mass of words, hardens into a permanent rift. Through his skill with language, his intelligence, his energy and industry, he becomes the Grand Panjandrum of the *New Yorker,* the American Earthquake itself. Privately he rages, storms, pouts, preens, demands and generally gets his own way—and he fills up his journals with his unhappiness, his continuing complaint that everything is going to hell in a basket, his petulance, his sense of personal betrayal by wives, children, family, associates. The Fifties become the Sixties; no Golden Years, these.

There is a willed financial irresponsibility to it all. Alfred Kazin notes the semi-pride he takes in not accumulating any money, and how, nailed by the I.R.S. for his failure to pay his income tax, he writes a book rationalizing that failure by claiming it is a protest against Big Government and the Cold War. He, Edmund Wilson, is too busy and important to have to bother to such details as filing his tax returns. It is the spoiled child all over again, punishing his mother for her failure to appreciate his genius and to pay his bills. As Kazin suggests, he has turned into a full-time curmudgeon. The conviction of his own rectitude has long since become a dominant working hypothesis. Earlier there was a ludicrous sequence in *Classics and Commercials* in which, not being addicted to detective mysteries himself, he pronounces them all abominably written, an absolute waste of time to read; it never enters his mind that personal taste might have anything to do with it.

He studies Russian, then proceeds to chastise Vladimir Nabokov, of all people, in print for his failures in translating Pushkin; in reply, the Russian-born Nabokov carves him up. He decides that Canada is what the United States ought to have been but wasn't, and uses that country's literature to indict his own country in a superficial display of petulance. He restores an old family place in upstate New York, begins spending his summers there; the fact that his fourth wife, Elena, whom he married in 1946 and stayed married to, detests it, is miserable when there, and after the early 1950s will not stay there with him, causes him no qualms. He will be the Squire of Talcottville, and if Elena can't handle it he will make do with what's available locally in the way of sex.

He spends a term at the Center for Advanced Studies at Wesleyan University; there are insufficient literary lights around to socialize with and to pay him homage—Moses Hadas, Dick Wilbur, Paul Horgan, Ihab Hassan, Jean Stafford, etc. Fortunately he can go to New York for the Christmas holidays: "After the blind little backwater of Middletown, the parties and gossip are quite intoxicating." And so on—902 pages plus glossary and index.

With all due awareness that *The Sixties* was written by the author of *Classics and Commercials, The Shores of Light,* and *Patriotic Gore,* this is about as fatuous, as sublimely self-infatuated, and for the most part as deadly tedious an exhibition in print as I've read any time recently. It's clear that when Wilson didn't have a subject-matter to develop, when he wasn't engaged in describing, analyzing, and explaining something outside of himself for the public to understand, he was both too self-infatuated and too naive about his own motives to have anything very interesting to report.

Naive? Vain? Consider the following. He is in Talcottville, and the wife of his dentist, who writes poetry and has shown herself to be fairly free with her favors, has come to consult him about her verse: "I don't understand her yen for me at my age, and I don't believe it was inspired by her finding out that, according to that list in *Esquire,* I was supposed to be one of the one hundred most important people in the world; she had already begun to show her interest in me."

Her inexplicable yen for him! One would think that *Vanity Fair* and *Madame Bovary* had never been written.

One can sympathize with him at the very end—his body deteriorating, a walk to the bathroom an ordeal. It would be easier if he didn't feel so sorry for himself. He died at Talcottville, June 12, 1972, age 77. Alfred Kazin and others have seen him as a survival of the old Anglo-American stock that once controlled the country—"the professional gentry of lawyers, preachers, educators, scientists, which from the time of New England's clerical oligarchs had remained the sustaining class of American intellectual life." Well, maybe, but the case seems less dynastic and more idiosyncratic to me. Having been brought up on the Wilson of the critical books, and come upon the journals only later, I am reminded less of the Oliver Wendell Holmes, Jr., of *Patriotic Gore*, as Kazin suggests, and more of the figure of the Wizard in the movie of *The Wizard of Oz*—one peeps behind the sound, fury, smoke, and jackanapes of the formidable facade and finds, desperately manipulating the console, Frank Morgan.

(1994)

An Honorable Profession:
H. L. Mencken of
the Baltimore Sunpapers

I think Fred Hobson has provided us, in his excellent biography of
H. L. Mencken (*Mencken: A Life,* 1994), with a very useful insight
into the Sage of Baltimore as journalist, when he notes of his
immersion in newspaper work that "he would always see himself
as a newspaperman (in a man's world) rather than the belletrist,"
and that "the profession of letters was permissible . . . because it was
entered through the door of rough turn-of-the-century metropolitan journalism."

I want to consider Mencken as a newsman. I do not intend, in
what follows, to try to psychoanalyze him, but rather to look at his
career and his work in terms of his involvement in newspaper journalism, which began within a couple of days after his father's death
in 1899, and closed only with the stroke that on November 23, 1948,
made it impossible for him to read or write any longer. His first newspaper story appeared in the Baltimore *Herald* for February 24, 1899,
a single paragraph about the theft of a horse, buggy and harness
worth $250 near Kingsville, Maryland; his last, for the Baltimore *Sun*
of November 9, 1948, was a column denouncing a law that prohib-
ited a group of whites and blacks from playing tennis together at
Druid Hill Park.

The two best books by far on being young and a newspaperman
during the Gutenberg Era, which ended with the arrival of the TV

set upon the American scene following World War II, are Mencken's
Newspaper Days (1941) and the second part of Theodore Dreiser's
A Book About Myself, likewise subtitled *Newspaper Days* (1922). They
are very different in kind. Dreiser's is intense, for the most part
humorless, very much in high earnest; Mencken's is light-hearted,
mirthful, and expansive—"mainly true, but with occasional stretch-
ers," as he noted in his preface.

Dreiser's book ends when, having worked as a reporter on newspapers in Chicago, St. Louis, and Pittsburgh, he moves to New York
City, finds himself unable to get anywhere writing on space rates
for the *World,* and decides that "come what might, this was the end
of newspaper reporting for me. Never again, if I died in the fight,
would I condescend to be a reporter on any paper. I might starve,
but if so—I would starve." Mencken's memoir closes with the fold-
ing of the *Herald* in 1906 after he had become its city editor, its managing editor, and for several months, editor-in-chief. His move to
the *Evening News* as news editor is remarked, and, less than two
months later, to the *Sun* as Sunday editor. I quote the final sentence
of *Newspaper Days:* "Since 1910, save for a brief and unhappy interlude in 1938, I have never had a newspaper job which involved the
control of other men's work, or any responsibility for it."

Upon finishing *Newspaper Days* in 1941, Mencken decided to write
an account of his years with the *Sunpapers,* not for publication during his lifetime but only "Later on, when time has released all con-
fidences and the grave has closed over all tender feelings . . . " That
manuscript, considerably pruned, has now been published as *Thirty-
five Years of Newspaper Work: A Memoir,* edited by Fred Hobson,
Vincent Fitzpatrick, and Bradford Jacobs (1994). I have to say that,
for all my interest in both author and subject—and I too began on
newspapers and even worked briefly for the *Sunpapers*—I found it
a rather disappointing affair, bearing qualitatively about the same
relationship to *Newspaper Days* as Mark Twain's more tedious works
such as *Following the Equator* do to *Huckleberry Finn* and the first

part of *Life on the Mississippi.* Nothing Mencken ever wrote could be devoid of internal life, but I do think that the other posthumous Mencken memoir, *My Life as Author and Editor,* which Jonathan Yardley edited (1993), is a far more interesting and important document.

Mencken, Dreiser, Mark Twain—these were but three among many American literary figures who began their careers in the newsroom, or, before the advent of the cylinder press and the linotype had made possible the large, staffed daily newspaper, the print shop. There were also Walt Whitman, William Dean Howells, Ernest Hemingway, George W. Cable, Ambrose Bierce, Joel Chandler Harris, Harold Frederic, Stephen Crane, David Graham Phillips, Henry Blake Fuller, Carl Sandburg, Ring Lardner, Willa Cather, Katherine Anne Porter, and so on up into our own time. Some of those cited also attended college; most did not.

When a young man went to work as a novice reporter of news, it was for meager pay. (Not until World War II and thereafter could a young woman usually hope to find a place in a newsroom other than with the society page.) Mencken hung around the newsroom of the Baltimore *Herald* for long days before receiving an assignment, and still longer before being given a job, at seven dollars a week and a trolley-car pass. Dreiser did the same at the Chicago *Globe* in 1892 before being taken on at $15 a week, which was what Hemingway received as a reporter when he began at the Kansas City *Star* in 1916.

The tradition of paying minuscule wages to aspiring journalists is of long standing. This I know from my own and my family's history. In or about the year 1910, one of my uncles, who later became a playwright and a screenwriter, worked for three months on the staff of the Charleston *News and Courier* in South Carolina for no pay at all, competing against another young man; the winner was to receive a job at $7 a week. The other fellow was a college graduate, and my uncle, who had only a seventh-grade education, lost out;

but a job came open in Birmingham, Alabama, and he went to work there. In my own instance, thirty-five years later in 1946 and after the currency inflation of two world wars, I started out on the Bergen *Evening Record* in New Jersey at $33 a week. Two years later, in the fall of 1948, when I quit the Associated Press and began graduate school at Johns Hopkins in Baltimore, one of my fellow students, a young man named Russell Baker, was working evenings as a police reporter on the *Sun* at $30 a week.

So it wasn't done for the money. Why, then, was a young man willing to labor long hours at low pay, in a profession that promised slow advancement and at best moderate recompense, in order to be a member of the working press? The motivation is obvious: because he wanted to *write* for a living. To be a newspaper reporter was a move in the direction of a career in letters. It was a way to work with words.

By that I do not mean that the youthful journalist saw himself as having to write newspaper stories because he could not earn a living writing fiction or poetry. Rather, the point is that in his mind the two modes were still largely undifferentiated. To understand what getting a job on a newspaper meant for Mencken and Dreiser, that point is important. In their day, and no doubt well into our own as well, it simply did not occur to most youths born into families without college backgrounds or close ties to the learned professions to make any hard-and-fast distinction between journalism and literature. To an extent that I think is no longer true, they were, or seemed to be, part and parcel of the same impulse.

The national letters reflect this. From the post–Civil War period onward into the era of Ernest Hemingway, an apprenticeship in the news often provided an entreé to the writing of fiction. The American novel was realistic, or naturalistic, in its aesthetic. Our literature was learning to include within its purview a far wider slice of everyday experience, particularly urban experience, than in the pre–Civil War decades. To make this new subject matter available for literary purposes, what was needed was an access to middle- and working-class life in terms of its own values, rather than those of an older, more elevated and polite cultural situation.

A necessary part of a writer's equipment was the ability to see and identify what was actually in place around him: the documentation of everyday life—i.e., journalism—became an important artistic tool. It has been said of William Dean Howells, who pioneered in American realism, that for him the absence of culture could be viewed only as a deprivation, whereas for Theodore Dreiser it was seen as a fact. Certainly this was true for Mencken. Although as Hobson notes in his biography, Mencken started off his literary career ensconced squarely within the Genteel Tradition in American letters, it wasn't too long before he was running interference for Dreiser and the writings of the early modernists in the columns of the *Smart Set* and the *Sun*. For about fifteen key years, from 1908 through the early 1920s, his principal cultural role was as Director of American Literary Implosion, which is to say, the person chiefly responsible for placing the dynamite charges that caused the obsolescent Literature of Ideality to collapse upon itself, and then shoveling away the debris so that the literature of the twentieth Century might have space to grow.

In fulfillment of that objective, Dreiser's *Sister Carrie* and *Jennie Gerhardt* proved to be extremely handy weapons for Mencken's use. "Ever since I began to find myself as a literary critic, in 1909," he recalled, "I had been on the lookout for an author who would serve me as a sort of tank in my war on the frauds and dolts who still reigned in American letters. It was not enough to ridicule and revile the fakers they admired and whooped up, though I did this with great enthusiasm; it was also necessary, if only for the sake of the dramatic contrast, to fight for writers, and especially for newcomers, they sniffed at—always provided, of course, these victims of their intransigent obtuseness really had something to offer." (*My Life as Author and Editor*)

Like Mencken, as a beginning newspaper reporter Dreiser was sent out each working day to confront the confusion, competitiveness, money-making, squalor, corruption, opportunism, extremes of wealth, racial and social admixture, and concentrated hubbub that made up everyday urban American experience. The contrast between what they encountered, and the version of life to be found in the approved literature of the Genteel Tradition, was striking. Dreiser, who was no man to see things evenhandedly, was astounded when a fellow journalist in St. Louis let him read a Zolaesque novel he and another man had written, but which, the friend said, "could never be published over here. We'd have to get it done abroad." Dreiser was indignant:

> You couldn't write about life as it was; you had to write about it as someone else thought it was, the ministers and farmers and dullards of the house. Yet here he was, as was I, busy in a profession that was hourly revealing that this sweetness and light code, this idea of a perfect world which contained neither sin nor shame for any save vile outcasts, criminals and vagrants, was the trashiest lie that was ever foisted upon an all too human world. Not a day, not an hour, but the pages of the very newspaper we were helping to fill with our scribbled observations were full of the most incisive pictures of the lack of virtue, honesty, kindness, even average human intelligence, not on the part of a few but of nearly everybody. (*Newspaper Days*)

Dreiser was appalled by what he saw around him; Mencken was—or at least would lead us to believe that he was—mainly intrigued and amused. Dreiser set out to make literature out of what he saw, and Mencken set out to see that Dreiser and others received the right to a full hearing and were not disqualified by virtue of either their choice of subject matter, as such, or their failure to moralize acceptably about it. For both of them, and for others whose entry onto the American literary scene came via the newsroom, what they saw as reporters led them to insist that the literary imagination of their time must not ignore or view obliquely the kind of everyday reality they had reported on—with the result that the Genteel Tradition crumbled and the literature of modernism could be written and published.

It is true, of course, that when the full fruition of that new literature arrived, so that the literature of genteel Ideality was set aside not only in subject matter but in language, form, and complexity of human portraiture, Mencken himself was largely unable to recognize it. He could, for example, accept and publish in the *Smart Set* several of the stories from James Joyce's *Dubliners,* yet say of *Ulysses* that it "seemed to me to be deliberately mystifying and mainly puerile, and I have never been able to get over a suspicion that Joyce concocted it as a kind of vengeful hoax." (*My Life as Author and Editor*)

Except for Dreiser, the handful of his American contemporaries whose fiction Mencken genuinely admired were not those whose work has lasted importantly beyond their day—Joseph Hergesheimer, Sinclair Lewis, James Branch Cabell (who still has his devotees, however few in number). But that is of small moment; there were other critics to champion and to teach us how to read modern literature, once the doors had been opened. Mencken it was who did most of all to pry them apart.

When he began his work the American literary firmament was dominated by William Dean Howells, Brander Matthews, Owen Wister, Henry Van Dyke, H. C. Boynton, Hamlin Garland, Robert Underwood Johnson, Edmund Clarence Stedman, Hamilton Wright Mabie, and Augustus Thomas—writers, as he said of a cluster of them after Howells's death, lacking "enough sin to raise a congressman's temperature one-hundredth of a degree" ("Want Ad"). By the time he lost interest, in the mid-1920s, Hemingway, Fitzgerald, Sherwood Anderson, Aiken, Faulkner, Eliot, Frost, Pound, Dos Passos, Williams, Marianne Moore, Ransom, Stevens, Cummings, and O'Neill were all publishing regularly.

Of those second-generation modernists, only Hemingway began on newspapers. It was the earlier generation, that of Mencken, Dreiser, Lardner, Stephen Crane, Phillips, Sandburg, etc., in whose beginnings the newsroom figured so prominently. For that first generation was needed to open up literature to urban experience, and also to detumesce the swollen literary idiom—purify the language of the tribe as it were—so that it could image that experience. Thus William Vaughn Moody, in "Ode in Time of Hesitation," an anti-imperialist poem, wanted to evoke the image of the midwestern metropolis where he lived and taught school: "Chicago sitteth at the northwest gates," he wrote. But Carl Sandburg began his poem about Chicago as follows: "Hog butcher to the world . . . "

What sets Mencken apart from those of his contemporaries who began in newsrooms, however, is that, unlike them, he remained a newspaperman all his working life. Except for periods during and briefly following American involvement in the two world wars, when he stopped writing for the *Sunpapers* because his views clashed with what he considered their pro-British editorial policy, he did not give up daily journalism once he had established himself on the national literary scene. Even when most actively engaged in New York, as editor of *The American Mercury,* he kept his residence in Baltimore and wrote his weekly pieces for the *Sun.* He covered the national political conventions, campaign tours, and other events, became a member of the company's board of directors, and even served as the *Sunpapers'* chief negotiator in its dealings with the American Newspaper Guild.

Clearly newspapers remained a major force in his life. He was Mencken of the *Sunpapers.* I think of that delicious moment at a press conference during the Progressive Party convention in 1948 when, or so the story goes as I heard it, Westbrook Pegler asked Henry Wallace about the so-called Guru letters he was alleged to have written, and Wallace replied that he would answer no questions put to him by Pegler or Pegler's stooges. Whereupon Mencken rose to his feet. "I'll ask the question," he declared. "I'm H. L. Mencken of the Baltimore *Sunpapers*." It was essential to the way that he viewed himself, a prime component of a proud man's self-esteem.

Now if, as I proposed earlier, the young men of Mencken's time and afterward strove for low-paying jobs in newspapers because it was a way of earning a living through writing, a first move toward a career in letters, then why didn't Mencken likewise give up daily journalism, once he had cleared away a secure and remunerative place for himself in the literary firmament? Now that he could write what he chose when he chose to do it, why did he persist in the remorseless, never-ending task of filling up columns of newsprint?

It certainly wasn't because of a passion for covering the news, as such. He soon tired of that—as did most of the young men and women who wrote for newspapers en route to literary careers. He ceased to take satisfaction in getting out a daily paper, did not wish to direct news coverage, lay out pages, write headlines, battle the composing room. From about 1908 onward Mencken was a commentator, not a reporter, and for the remainder of his days on earth it was the expression of his opinion, not the gathering of news, that concerned him.

He remained a newspaperman because he liked to sound off, to make a noise. In that respect he did not, in one sense, differ from any other person who has written for a living, whether fiction or fact, prose or poetry. And what he wrote about the underlying motive for authorship held for himself: " . . . an author, like any other so-called artist, is a man in whom the normal vanity of all men is so vastly exaggerated that he finds it a sheer impossibility to hold it in. His overpowering impulse is to gyrate before his fellow men, flapping his wings and emitting defiant yells. This being forbidden by the police in all civilized countries, he takes it out by putting his yells on paper." ("The Fringes of Lovely Letters")

But there were particular compulsions at work within him that made it vital that he do his sounding-off in newsprint. I pledged myself earlier not to get into the business of psychoanalyzing the Sage of Baltimore (I have had a go at it elsewhere), so I will remark only on a few of the various needs that propelled him along his way, without attempting to inquire into why they might have done so. These were: (1) the need to demonstrate that, although possessing intense artistic leanings, he was no dreamy esthete, but an eminently practical and worldly-wise fellow; (2) the need and wish to smite self-righteous authority figures; (3) the need to insist upon the absolute futility of any attempt to ameliorate the human condition, whether social, political, intellectual, or moral; and (4) the need to feel himself in control of the situation, and to slap down anything and anybody appearing to menace that control.

Such needs existed not in separation but in creative relation to and as part and parcel of one another. For Mencken, however, their combined thrust meant that he couldn't cut loose from his role as newspaper columnist—not even in the 1920s when the *American Mercury* was in full flower and he was happily battling prohibitionists, book and magazine censors, anti-evolutionists, American Legionnaires, the British Empire, Calvin Coolidge, chiropractors, believers in Christian Endeavor, and all other Right Thinking people everywhere. Each Monday his *Evening Sun* column kept the animals stirred up and reasserted his presence on the home front.

It is frequently said of him—he several times allowed as much himself—that he enjoyed and welcomed adverse criticism, did not take it personally, maintained a cheerful distinction between criticism and critic, held no grudges, and habitually let bygones be bygones. That is what he wished us to believe. To an extent there was truth in it. Yet the author of several memoirs designed for publication only long after his death, in which he reviewed the various controversies in which he had engaged and proclaimed all who differed from him to be either knaves or imbeciles, was scarcely engaged in permitting bygones to remain bygones. Moreover, any man who would edit and publish a book containing 132 pages of epithets directed at himself (*Menckeniana: a Schimpflexikon,* 1928) was almost certainly impelled to demonstrate something about his ability to take it.

The traumatic event of Mencken's adult life was what happened to him just before and during the First World War. In any assessment of his career the impact of that catastrophe, the abrupt check it gave to his newly burgeoning journalistic career, forcing him to give up his weekly column because of his pro-German, anti-British sentiments, placing him at odds not merely with the rank and file of readers but with the owners, publishers, and controlling directors of the *Sunpapers,* cannot be overstated. He was told to mind his manners and button his lip. (I am reminded of that line by Ring Lardner: " Shut up he explained.")

All he could do was stay quiet and bide his time, which he did. But almost every one of the stands that he took in the 1920s and thereafter, almost every position he assumed on every public issue, was formidably reinforced by what happened from 1915 through 1918. The celebrated *Boobus Americanus,* it should be remembered, voted for Woodrow Wilson, served in the A.E.F., and afterward joined the American Legion. Wilson, who led America's involvement in the "war to end wars," was the supreme highminded moralist and Presbyterian elder of his day, and, moreover, a southerner. No section of the United States was more avid for a declaration of war in 1917 than the southern states. The Prohibition Amendment, enacted during the war, outlawed the sale of beer, a beverage brewed principally by German-Americans. The American language was decidedly *not* the British language. And so on.

I do not mean by this, of course, that many or even most of the quintessential Menckenian attitudes were not in place before the coming of the war, for demonstrably they were. But what happened during the war intensified and hardened them. With the return of what President Harding termed Normalcy, Mencken moved back onto center stage, but with an agenda and a hit list.

An important reason why Mencken remained a newspaperman was that turning out his weekly column was central to his way of writing and thinking. For someone of his temperament and abundant energies, the sequence of publication he evolved was almost ideally adapted to his needs. His weekly column for the *Evening Sun* and his coverage of the political party conventions kept him in close touch with the national political scene and enabled him to sound off on whatever came to mind. He could then refine and develop those impressions for the *American Mercury* and include the best, even further touched up, in the *Prejudices* books; or else develop, combine, and adapt them for full-length books such as *Notes on Democracy* (1926) and *Treatise on the Gods* (1930).

He wrote his newspaper pieces, from all accounts, rapidly and well; at the political conventions, knocking out his stories hunt-and-peck on his portable typewriter, he produced copy that needed little editing. What he did with it later, for magazine and book use, was principally by way of intensifying the language and sharpening the wit. We can watch the process as it took place, through the collection of his newspaper stories assembled by Marion Elizabeth Rodgers, *The Impossible H. L. Mencken* (1991), and the subsequent development of some of them in the *Prejudices* volumes and his full-length books.

It should be pointed out that the Mencken who survives and to an extent even flourishes today, seven decades and more after his heyday in the 1920s and almost a half-century after he stopped writing, is not the author of the full-length treatises, or even of the *Days* books—although I must say that I cannot imagine *Happy Days* and especially *Newspaper Days* ever going without readers. It is the essayist who has lasted best, the author of those medium-length pieces most of which were originally newspaper columns and that crackle so with wit and sarcasm. Each reader will have his or her favorites, whether "The Sahara of the Bozart"; "Want Ad," the farewell to

William Dean Howells; "Professor Veblen," the hilarious assault on the author of *Theory of the Leisure Class;* "In Memoriam: W. J. B.," the Bryan obituary; the discourse on "Gamalielese"; "The Divine Afflatus"; "Imperial Purple"; the memoir of Huneker; "The Husbandman," with that marvelous sentence: "There, where the cows low through the still night, and the jug of Peruna stands behind the stove, and bathing begins, as at Biarritz, with the vernal equinox—there is the reservoir of all the nonsensical legislation which now makes the United States a buffoon among the great nations." Or others; I cite my own favorites from among so many that are splendid.

Do I believe what the author is maintaining in such gems of vituperation? Sometimes yes, sometimes not at all; but what does that matter? Does one agree with Samuel Johnson's prejudices most of the time? Johnson provides an apt comparison; the similarities are intriguing. Indeed, it seems to me quite likely that, just as with Ursa Major, Mencken's eventual place will be that of a personality, as much as for what he wrote. In Hobson's words, "it is entirely possible that he is one of those writers, like Dr. Johnson or Thomas Carlyle or Henry Adams, whose *life,* both as fact and as metaphor, will always inspire as much interest as his work" (*Mencken: A Life*).

What are Mencken's best pieces, as has been so often noted, but consummate works of humor? Not for the television masses, to be sure, but for the reader who can grasp the compacted insult contained in a line such as that from "Want Ad," concerning President Nicholas Murray Butler of Columbia University: "Moreover, he is a member of the American Academy himself, elected as a wet to succeed Edgar Allan Poe." If in years to come there will be few who will know what a wet was, or the relationship of the American Academy of Poe's day to the dying Genteel Tradition, or what Nicholas Murray Butler had to do with either, the loss will be theirs.

Frequently one hears the lament, "If only H. L. Mencken were alive today—," meaning that there is abundant humbug around that cries out for the Sage's genius at castigation. The Messrs. Hobson, Fitzpatrick, and Jacobs echo it in the introduction of *Thirty-five Years of Newspaper Work*. What they and everyone else uttering such a lament overlook is the fact that not only would it be impossible to bring off in our day, but that by the 1930s and 1940s, Mencken himself couldn't bring it off.

The archetypal Menckenian iconoclasm and demolition we so cherish dates almost exclusively from the 1910s and 1920s. Once the Depression got into high gear and Hitler took over in Germany. it became no longer possible to position oneself in print as above the melee, or as Mencken put it, "Well-fed, unhounded by sordid cares, at ease in Zion" ("On Being an American"). His act was over. Read Mencken on the New Deal, on the C.I.O. vs. the automobile companies, on the Blitz, on the need to repeal the Neutrality Act— if, that is, you can find what he wrote, for the numerous collections of his work, whether by himself or by others, include few such pieces. The Mencken touch didn't work then, nor would it work today. I have known political columnists who had the Menckenian style down perfectly, and could use the Sage's rhetorical tactics to a fare-thee-well. Yet they couldn't achieve the Menckenian effect, for the same reason that he couldn't manage it, either, once the banks failed, the breadlines formed, and the concentration camps were set up; what was happening mattered too much. There was too much at stake.

Not surprisingly, the Mencken of the later 1930s and the 1940s was a largely disappointed man. He focussed his discontent upon the political scene, but his anger over what was wrong with nation and world was at bottom an emblem for his personal unhappiness and frustration. The refrain that runs through the later chapters of Mencken's *Thirty-five Years of Newspaper Work* is the alleged failure of the *Sun* to develop into the "the really great newspaper that it might have been." What the failure appears to have consisted of, one gathers from reading both that work and the entries in the *Diary of H. L. Mencken* edited by Charles A. Fecher and published in 1989, was the refusal of the management to compel the editors of the *Sun* and the *Evening Sun* to oppose almost everything that President Franklin D. Roosevelt and the New Deal undertook to do domestically, to protest Roosevelt's efforts to aid a beleaguered England against the Nazis, and to attack him for seeking to lead the nation into war. In other words, to adopt the political and social views of H. L. Mencken.

Thus the president of the *Sunpapers,* Paul Patterson, "was not equal to the task of formulating and enforcing a really enlightened editorial policy. His interest in the editorial pages was always very slight and seldom more than intermittent: he gave his chief attention to the news department, or to such coney-catching features as the comic section." All others in the *Sunpapers* hierarchy—John Owens, Hamilton Owens, Harry Black, Gerald Johnson, Frank Kent, Philip Wagner, the papers' collection of "third-rate editorial writers"—were hopeless. Again and again Mencken sounded off in such fashion. As Charles Fecher remarks in his introduction to the *Diary:* "One has a mental picture of Paul Patterson, the dignified president of the *Sunpapers,* diving under his desk when he hears Mencken coming down the hall so he won't have to listen to another tirade about the 'imbecility' of the editorial page." (*Thirty-five Years*)

By that time, Mencken had ceased to be an active participant in the national letters. He had virtually lost all interest in literature by the mid-1920s, had given up editorship of the *American Mercury* in 1933, moved back into the Hollis Street house in which he had grown up, and no longer made regular trips to New York City. He went daily to his office at the *Sun,* took part in *Sunpapers* deliberations, fumed over politics and the war, wrote his memoirs, and kept his work on the American language up to date. In short, by the 1940s H. L. Mencken, widowed and in his sixties, was back where he had started out, his attitudes and opinions still largely and doggedly those which he had formed when young. He would become increasingly frustrated and bewildered by what was happening within a city, a nation, a world, and a newspaper organization that declined to stay in place.

His last years, after the stroke of late 1948, were a dreadful caricature, as it were, of the preceding decade. Now he literally couldn't articulate his opinions. No Dante, prescribing appropriate punishment for the sinners in the *Inferno,* could have devised a more hideous conclusion for this man, of all men. In his own words, spoken to a departing visitor, "It's a hell of a state of things when the only thing a man can read or write is his name."

Fred Hobson's summation is to the point:

> Devastating as the results of Mencken's stroke were, they were probably made even worse by the manner in which he received them. Not only might another patient have adjusted better to the inability to read and write—one whose entire life had not been devoted to those pursuits—but another patient, one of Mencken's doctors later suggested, probably would have accepted with better grace the inability to speak with facility. Among other things, Mencken was a victim of that great pride, as well as an aversion to social embarrassment, that he had always possessed. From his youth he had been orderly, precise, competent in all he undertook—above all, *in control*—and if he could not now do things well, he sometimes refused to do them at all.

No longer in control. That was what so enraged and dismayed him— just as it had in those years when he had been forced to work in his father's cigar business and had even contemplated suicide until liberated by his father's death; and during World War I when his pan-Germanism got him muzzled; and in the New Deal and World War II years when no one in authority, whether in Washington or on the *Sunpapers,* would heed his remonstrances. His response at all such times was to dig in his heels, to intensify his opposition, to adhere ever more atavistically and furiously to his loyalties and prejudices—to concede nothing.

In William Manchester's words, "He feared change and battled it to the end." ("Mencken in Person," in John Dorsey, ed., *On Mencken*, 1980.) He was not in control. And when contradicted, he was recalcitrant as a mule.

Earlier I posed the question of why it was that Mencken, unlike his other literary contemporaries who began on newspapers, did not move on to a full-time existence as litterateur, but remained in newspaper journalism. I suggested that it was because he needed a place to sound off, and that writing his newspaper column gave him a matchless opportunity to do just that. There were other reasons as well for his remaining a working newspaperman, not the least of them being that he was very, very good at it. "I am at my best in articles written in heat and printed at once," he said of himself, and if that is not quite true, for he is at his best in those articles as embellished and intensified through revision for book publication, setting down that first impassioned impression for newspaper publication was certainly an essential dimension of his artistry.

I think that more than most good writers, it was necessary that the one-man show he put on feature him directly and personally, and the weekly newspaper column permitted him to do that with the minimum amount of contrivance and dissimulation, right there in the city where he was born and grew up. The trait was spotted early on, by no less an authority on journalistic showmanship than Colonel Henry Watterson, the old-time editor of the Louisville *Courier-Journal* and Democratic Party warrior from the days of Samuel J. Tilden and Grover Cleveland onward: "Think of it! The staid old Baltimore *Sun* has got itself a Whangdoodle. Nor is it one of those bogus Whangdoodles which we sometimes encounter in the sideshow business—merely a double-cross between a Gin-Rickey and a Gyascutis—but a genuine, guaranteed, imported direct from the mountains of Hepsidam." (Quoted in William Manchester, *H. L. Mencken: Disturber of the Peace,* 1951)

To merit the notice of a Marse Henry Watterson, and the attention of politicos, newspaper editors, braumeisters, cops, and other men of affairs in the world of power and civic renown, was no trivial consideration for a young man who had been taught to believe, and ever afterward suspected and even perhaps feared, that there was something impractical and sissyish about an addiction to books and literature. There is the oft-cited boast from the preface to *Newspaper Days:* "At a time when the respectable bourgeois youngsters of my generation were college freshmen, oppressed by simian sophomores and affronted with balderdash daily and hourly by chalky pedagogues, I was at large in a wicked seaport of half a million people, with a front seat at every public show, as free of the night as of the day, and getting earfuls and eyefuls of instruction in a hundred giddy arcana, none of them taught in schools. . . . if I neglected the humanities I was meanwhile laying in all the worldly wisdom of a police lieutenant, a bartender, a shyster lawyer, or a midwife."

He entered literature via journalism, then, and as Hobson notes, that made it all right, because journalism was rough and masculine. To cut himself off entirely from newspapers, to discard that identity as H. L. Mencken of the *Sunpapers,* was to lose touch with the Real, as he saw it. He associated his literary existence with New York City, and his newspaper identity with Baltimore, and important though the literary life was, it was not what mattered most. The Proustian notion that the only ultimate reality is art, and that whatever exists in time is finally ephemeral and meaningless, would never do for him.

In this respect, the piece he wrote comparing the two places, entitled "On Living in Baltimore," is interesting. "The very richest man, in New York," he contends, "is never quite sure that the house he lives in now will be his next year. . . . The intense crowding in the town, and the restlessness and unhappiness that go with it, make it almost impossible for anyone to accumulate the materials of a home. . . . The charm of getting home, as I see it, is the charm of getting back to what is inextricably my own—to things familiar and long loved, to things that belong to me alone and none other. I have lived in one house in Baltimore for nearly forty-five years. . . . It is as much a part of me as my two hands. If I had to leave it I'd be as certainly crippled as if I lost a leg." Baltimore was where he *lived;* whatever else he might do or say or write, he was H. L. Mencken of the Baltimore *Sunpapers.*

I close on a personal note. I first discovered the joys of Mencken through the *Days* books, which I read in the early morning hours of midsummer, 1949, after getting off work on the copy desk of the Wilmington, Delaware, *Morning News.* The nights that summer were suffocatingly hot, the hottest I have ever known; editing news stories and putting headlines on them was terribly boring, and I longed to be able to go back full-time to Baltimore and the Writing Seminars (they were not called that then) of the Johns Hopkins University, where I could teach a course and edit the *Hopkins Review* and be among literary folk again. By September I could take no more, and I headed back down U.S. 40.

I too had originally set out to be a newspaperman, and I worked as reporter, city editor, and desk man for several years before going to graduate school. But, except for a brief interlude as an editorial writer in the mid-1950s, thereafter I made my career on college campuses, and I have never regretted it. Even so, for most of the years of my adult life I have always maintained some kind of a newspaper connection, whether as editor of book pages or writer of columns, and I still do an occasional piece. So I think I can understand, if on a diminished scale, something of the attraction that writing for newspapers had for H. L. Mencken.

He told Bill Manchester, when he went to work for the *Sun* in 1947, "You'll love it, but be sure you get out before you're thirty-five." ("Mencken in Person"). If in so advising, Mencken was implicitly second-guessing the choices he had made in his own career, then surely he was drawing the wrong conclusions. To think of Mencken, what he was, what he wrote, the role he played in the national letters, without the *Sunpapers* affiliation is impossible. As well think of Winston Churchill without the House of Commons, or Lucrezia Borgia without access to a supply of poison. "Whatever Mencken was, he was a journalist," Fred Hobson declares, and rightly so.

As Mencken himself wrote in the Preface to *A Mencken Chrestomathy* (1949) not long before undergoing the stroke that did him in as a writer, "I do not regret that I gave so much of my time and energy, especially in my earlier years, to this journalism, for I had a swell time concocting it, and in its day it got some attention. . . . There is something delightful about getting an idea on paper while it is still hot and charming, and seeing it in print before it begins to pale and stale." Anyone who has ever sat around in a newsroom and, when a copy boy brought the first edition up from the pressroom and handed out copies of the still-warm newsprint, opened the pages to scan his own words transformed into print, will know what Mencken meant by that.

In summation: he was a working newspaperman, the very best in the business. Journalism was his profession. It was an honorable profession, and he practiced it with enduring distinction.

(1995)

Our Absolutely Deplorable Literary Situation—and Some Thoughts on How to Fix It Good

I open this chronicle of Literary Frustration with a disclaimer. This is, that I am not ordinarily given to gloomy prognostication, and have always suspected most such laments as being at bottom variations on the age-old theme of the Death of the Gods. Yet notwithstanding that, I have to say that the American literary situation as it is shaping up nowadays is, to anyone who believes that literature is something more than diversionary reading, enough to drive a prudent person to strong drink.

I propose to deal in practical, not theoretical terms, focussing my resentment not on problems of spiritual malaise, cultural degeneration, the failure of the center to hold, and the like, but on such mundane matters as readership, audience, and commerce in general. For if good books cannot get published because the publishing houses are concentrating on better-paying junk, and if it is impossible for readers to find out about worthy new books because these seldom get reviewed, then what chance will even the most accomplished young contemporary author have to get a book before the public?

From the standpoint of getting good books published and read, the belles-lettres, as we used to call them, are in woeful shape and getting worse. Poetry, as an artistic genre meant to be read by persons other than one's fellow poets, is dead in the market. Fiction of a literary kind is still breathing, but the prognosis is melancholy. As for criticism—well, in the sense of having anything to do with the function of helping to sort out and make accessible what is being written by working poets and novelists, it scarcely even exists any more. It now looks, I regret to say, as if Marshall McLuhan was correct; the Age of Gutenberg is rapidly on the way out, having been succeeded by the Age of the Television Set.

What is happening is as follows:

1. More money can be made in pop culture—i.e., television, middlebrow costume romance, mass market paperbacks, assorted gimmickry, etc.—than in literature.

2. Because the commercial medium whereby literature is produced and sold is the same as those whereby the artifacts of popular culture are marketed, the profit-and-loss performance of literature is being evaluated by people who are chiefly in business to sell mass market cultural products. It is as if the choice of titles to be issued by the Cuala Press had been left up to the publishers of the Guinness Book of Records.

3. Literature today, in short, is more or less in the situation of a motherless adolescent whose father has since remarried and whose stepmother doesn't much care for the presence of teen-agers around the house.

The outcome of such a happenstance is inevitable. As noted, poetry is comatose, and literary fiction is stumbling. The TV tube is in large measure responsible for this, because it has virtually obliterated the common ground that once existed between literature and pop culture. Today it is either Judith Krantz or Eudora Welty, John Jakes or John Barth. There is little or no overlap any more, for the reason that the expectations of the general audience have been tailored to the aesthetic dimensions of the TV set. Why bother to sort out and explore the emotional and intellectual subtleties of one's response to a novel, when television can make everything so simple, clear, and direct?

Except for what can be managed through snob appeal—not an

inconsiderable factor in the spread of culture, to be sure—it has become extremely difficult to sell good literary fiction to a large audience, and it isn't going to get any easier in the years to come. For, to repeat, by removing the experience of complexity in culture, television is adulterating the aesthetic taste of all but the more resolute and dedicated readers.

The result is that we are coming to have two kinds of audiences— a small, mostly academic audience; and a vast, middlebrow, commercial audience. The former is served by little magazines, literary quarterlies, university presses, and certain small publishing houses, most of them without national distribution in most bookstores. The latter, which reads no poetry or criticism and only some fiction, is serviced by the same publication outlets that sell books and magazines to the mass audience.

The middlebrow clientele can still be persuaded to buy certain literary works if these are cleverly packaged and prominently endorsed by TV celebrities. But it is cultural sleight-of-hand; read this novel because Barbara Walters says it's good. The analogy is with persuading people to buy chocolate-coated cookies as a way of supporting the Girl Scouts of America.

The magazines that used to span the gap between highbrow and middle—the *New Yorker, Harper's,* the *Atlantic,* etc.—no longer do so. They have gone over to the middlebrows and now strive to provide reading matter designed for use before and after watching television.

Under these circumstances, what has happened is that the literary practitioner coming onto the scene today faces the option of either retreating into the academy or else becoming a branch of show business. On the one hand, there is a literature written for and read by literary professionals alone; on the other, there is fiction published and marketed according to the star system. Those authors who seem potentially exploitable as celebrities are given essentially the same kind of promotion as Hollywood figures and presidential

candidates, and then judged by how well they can conduct themselves in the spotlight—i.e., as public entertainers. A novelist who
is unwilling or unable to embark on an extensive author's tour, or
who can't be made to perform colorfully on a network talk show,
is out of it; he or she had better go looking for a teaching position.

How, other than through use of the techniques of applied showbiz,
can an author of a new book hope to get it noticed and read? By
good reviews? The odds are heavily against it. Compare the book
review situation now to what it was even as recently as a few decades
ago. A novel coming out in the 1940s and 1950s, if it were more than
usually promising, might well receive three reviews in publications
with other than regional circulation—in the *New York Times Book
Review,* the *Herald-Tribune Books* supplement, and the *Saturday
Review.* If one of the three chose not to review the book, or if its
review was uncomprehending and dismissive, the book still had two
other chances at being properly noticed. Moreover, the news-mag-
azines reviewed lots of books each week; the *Atlantic* and *Harper's*
were still literary rather than Beautiful People publications; and both
the *New Republic* and the *Nation* had strong book sections edited
by literary figures of genuine stature.

Today the *Trib* and the *Saturday Review* are gone. The only newspaper of national circulation that makes a substantial effort to cover
the book publishing scene is the *Times.* In point of fact it does its
best; habitually it leans over backwards not to be provincial or ultra-
commercial. But it can only review so many books per week, and
its failure to review a book can wreck that book's chances.

There is the *New York Review of Books,* but it is utterly unconcerned with new fiction, and its provincialism is almost beyond
belief. *USA Today* devotes scarcely more serious attention to books
than it does to stamp collecting; it has only a scant literary presence.
The *Village Voice* is a scruffy affair designed to be read by the patrons

of unisex hair salons. *Harper's?* The *Atlantic?* As well look for coverage of a new novel in the *Daily Racing Form.* The *New Republic* and the *Nation?* They have long since ceased to count for anything much in the literary cosmos.

The melancholy fact is that, other than getting a prominent review in the New York *Times,* which is possible but unlikely, the only way that a good novel by an unknown writer can receive any attention, other than of a local or at most regional nature, is to get noticed on National Public Radio. But that is a dubious proposition, because NPR is a branch of the entertainment industry, and those in charge of selecting the books to be spotlighted are looking for "angles"— i.e., controversial or off-the-beaten-track content, not literary mastery.

I have been discoursing principally in terms of the obstacles faced by unpublished fiction writers. When it comes to poets, then there is no hope at all—for there is simply no such thing as a national audience reading poetry any more, nor has there been for at least a quarter-century. It is a cottage industry, with the clientele mainly drawn from the immediate geographical area. No consensus exists; good poets who have published a half-dozen or more volumes cannot assume that their new work will be noticed and reviewed, anywhere.

Almost all the commercial book publishing houses have long since given up bringing out collections of new poems; university presses and small imprints now do the book publishing. The poets earn their livelihood by giving readings, teaching, and collecting fellowships. The few big national prizes are largely controlled by a handful of poets and hangers-on clustered mainly in and around Morningside Heights. But to win a Pulitzer or Bollingen Prize for verse doesn't remotely mean what it once did, anyway. No longer do readers go rushing to the book stores in search of the winning volumes when the announcements are made. If they did, they'd not be apt to find them, for the simple reason that most stores don't stock new verse any more. The practice of poetry has never been a particularly prestigious affair, but nowadays it is at close to rock bottom in public presence. It reminds me somehow of ice fishing. You have to want to go fishing awfully badly to do it at all.

As for criticism, which is to say, writings about writing, we have the odd spectacle of an intense academic interest in literary theory, and almost none, academic or otherwise, in understanding, evaluating, and sorting out the literature being written today. Newspaper book reviews are the beginning and the end of it. The literary role that used to be played by the magazine critics—i.e., Mencken in the *Mercury*, Cowley in the *New Republic*, Krutch in the *Nation*, etc.—doesn't get played any more. Except for a few newspaper critics such as Yardley in the *Washington Post*, the idea that there could be a coherent, identifiable critical viewpoint about contemporary letters, articulated in a single place and offering consistent commentary on the literary scene, appears to be as dated as the *feuilleton* and the Reo Flying Cloud.

To return again to the novel, which at least maintains some pretense of literary vitality and general interest, consider the plight of the young writer, without influential connections and without an established literary agent, who hopes to break into print. The day when such a person could mail off a manuscript to one of the big trade publishing houses, and, if possessing talent, expect to have that talent recognized and editorial guidance offered to bring it to fruition, has almost totally vanished from ken. Many of the big houses won't even read unsolicited manuscripts. Or if they do keep a recent Fairleigh Dickinson graduate on the payroll to glance at what comes in over the transom, they still rely primarily upon what is sent them by literary agents.

The missing element in today's book publishing, from the standpoint of the young author hoping to get a book accepted is, simply, *editing*. This is because the economics of the industry will no longer accommodate the system whereby so many of our best American writers got their first books published and their careers launched. The kind of editor who takes pride in identifying potential literary merit in the fumbling manuscript of an unknown young author, and in working with that author over a period of time, often through several drafts, to bring that potential talent to fruition, is as rare nowadays as Leopold Bloom's roc's auk's egg.

Unless a book is already in close to publishable form when submitted, few editors would dare take a chance on it. To spend numerous hours reading successive drafts and writing lengthy directives for a first novel that will very likely lose money when published, whatever the future prospects of the author, is no way to hold onto an editorial job in trade publishing today. Nobody in a position of authority is going to be at all impressed by the thought that, red ink notwithstanding, a potentially distinguished literary talent is being brought along.

To offer a young author a modest option on a book, much less an actual contract to publish, an editor must first gain the approval of an editorial committee. Given the configuration of big-time trade publishing today, the deciding vote will very likely be cast by the senior editor, who has just negotiated a contract, with a $750,000 advance, for a still-to-be-written history of the sex life of the Kennedy family, including in-laws, and is already under fire from the soap company conglomerate owning the house for having failed to turn a profit for two successive seasons.

Do I exaggerate unduly? If you think so, examine the book trade news in successive issues of *Publishers Weekly* for a month or so. There you will see what publishing is mostly about in our time. As for the shades of Max Perkins, Hiram Haydn, Alfred Knopf, John Farrar, Ferris Greenslet, Alfred Harcourt, Ben Huebsch, Jim Henle, etc., if any such were brought back to life and asked to listen in on an editorial staff conclave at most of the big houses today, they would believe themselves to be not at a book publishing meeting in New York City but a marketing session on the MGM lot in Culver City, California.

Thus the function of the editor in the post-Gutenberg Era. Add to this the fact that, as noted earlier, if the young novelist's book does get accepted, properly edited, and published, the chances of its receiving the kind of serious reviews that will call it forcefully to the attention of a sizeable number of readers are quite poor, particularly if the publisher can't also find a prominent TV or radio personality to testify on its behalf. What we have, in sum, is about as sour a future outlook for our country's literature as has existed since James Fenimore Cooper first began publishing fiction in the early 1820s.

What then, as V. I. Lenin once remarked under somewhat different circumstances, is to be done?

Agèd and overweight though I am, I have even so a few ideas to put forth. A decent Respect to the Opinions of Mankind, however, requires that they be accompanied by a declaration of the assumptions under which they have been formulated. To wit:

I believe that a decent-sized audience for good literature—call it elitist if you will—does indeed exist, and that potentially it is considerably larger than the mostly academic audience that currently supports the quarterly reviews and little magazines. Nor is it identical with the audience for avant-garde literature, though the latter can comprise part of it. The distinguishing characteristic of this elite audience is that it *prefers* reading books to watching TV each evening. As a book-buying clientele it is probably sizeable enough, and affluent enough, to support the national letters without the help of the mass entertainment industry, and without retreat into the academy.

Very well. Given those hypotheses, what needs to be done?

1. First of all, the audience for good literature must be approached as a decisive entity in itself, not as the intellectual or literary fringe of the mass middlebrow audience. In order for this to happen, it must be identified, singled out, and carefully cultivated.

2. Literature, if it is to survive and flourish, cannot continue to be operated as a subsidiary branch of the cookbook and 900-telephone-number industry. The publication and dissemination of good literature must be *separated*—physically, geographically, culturally, financially—from the publication and dissemination of items of interest to devotees of mass TV culture.

3. We have got to establish, or re-establish, a *literary situation* which is not part of and not dependent upon the spare venture capital of the purveyors of cultural pablum.

4. To do that, we must foment a revival of intelligent criticism of contemporary literature and of literary journalism about it, so as to provide focus and cohesion.

5. The key to the whole situation is to establish several first-class nationally distributed magazines—not literary magazines, mind you, but general-circulation magazines designed for an educated, intelligent, sophisticated audience—which as part of their operation would regularly review and criticize a range of new books (including new poetry).

6. In order to bring all this off (i.e., to rejuvenate the national letters), a full-fledged conspiracy is needed. Those who believe that the American literary imagination is worth preserving must be encouraged to master the same kind of proselytizing zeal with which other conspiratorial groups such as the National Rifle Association, the Church of Jesus Christ of Latter-Day Saints, the Republican Party, and the American Kennel Club approach the influencing of public opinion.

Is any of the above likely to happen? I give it about the same chance as that of the Chevrolet Division of General Motors in producing an American-manufactured automobile that will merit and receive a "better-than-average" frequency-of-repair rating in the *Consumer Reports Buying Guide.* Which is to say, next to none at all. It is not only improbable; it is wildly visionary. Set next to it, *transition*'s famed "Revolution of the Word" of the 1920s seems eminently practical.

Yet if our letters are to flourish, it, or something like it will have to be done. The key, as noted earlier, is probably Item No. 5, above. What this country's literature badly needs is several well-edited periodicals (none of them either edited in or funded through New York City), published on a monthly basis or more frequently, and offering articles, familiar essays, stories, poems, etc., directed at a "highbrow," but *not* merely academic or avant-garde, audience. By this I decidedly do not mean literary magazines as such; nor do I have in mind what quarterly reviews do. They would range the spectrum of civilized curiosity, but do so for an intelligent, sophisticated audience which enjoys reading about topics other than lawn care, antiques, and the domestic arrangements of film stars. The objective would be to produce the kind of magazine journalism that persons who like to read would read for pleasure.

Where now is the magazine that provides interesting, well-written fare for an educated and sophisticated general audience? Or put it this way: other than in specialized publications, how many good magazine articles have *you* read recently? Would you subscribe to a periodical of a non-academic, non-professional nature that offered a regular array of pieces about various topics, pieces that neither insulted your intelligence nor strove constantly to be modish and trendy? (This last is one reason why the magazines I propose have got to be edited outside the corporate limits of the Big Apple.) And as part of such a periodical, wouldn't you welcome some sensible and insightful commentary about new books, written not for academic specialists alone but for intelligent, educated readers?

Think what the existence of a few such magazines would do for our culture. Regularly published and imaginatively edited, they would develop and maintain a solid and devoted audience of intelligent readers which, though not large by mass media standards, would be quite numerous enough—and consequential enough— to provide a foundation for a lively literary and cultural situation. Our writers would be able to get their books intelligently reviewed, in publications sufficiently important and widely enough circulated so that favorable critical appraisal would carry real meaning at independent, if not at chain, bookstores.

In saying that our literature must separate itself from the book and magazine industry of the metropolitan Northeast, what I mean is that it has got to be able to function on terms that do not require it to compete with the commercial mass market expectations of the entertainment industry, centered as the latter are on the television audience. The only way to arrange that is to operate independently of it. And that cannot be done as things now stand, because the two industries, publishing and showbiz-TV, are too massively and intricately tied together, up and down the line.

To state the proposition in book-business terms, obviously considerably more money is to be made from promoting a book so that it will sell 100,000 copies instead of 25,000, than from promoting a book so that it will sell 10,000 copies instead of 5,000. No publishing house, especially if owned by a conglomerate, is going to try to do both. That is why the deck is now so cruelly stacked against literary publishing. What the future welfare of our literature depends upon is the kind of book publishing that will *concentrate* on doing the latter rather than the former.

It comes down, then, simply to this: so-called print culture must be removed from the auspices of the TV-centered mass entertainment industry. It is too valuable to be allowed to go by default—which is what is happening now. We are letting it dwindle away toward oblivion. It does not follow, either logically or practically, that because many more people regularly watch Oprah Winfrey than read Annie Dillard or Mark Helprin, literature is therefore doomed. But when we allow the same industry to preside over the promulgation, distribution, and critical evaluation of all three, as if they were equally engaged in showbiz, what chance do the latter two have?

We must therefore dissolve the Financial Bands that have connected contemporary letters with the popular entertainment industry and let literature flourish on its own, as the product of literary folks writing for a literary audience.

We come now to the question of how it is to be done, and who is to pick up the tab for doing it. There you have me, for I haven't the slightest idea. Having identified the cat and explained why and how it is to be belled, I leave the belling to others more resourceful than myself.

I will say this, however. What the enterprise probably needs is a Rebel Angel, someone with lots and lots of dough, addicted psychologically to swimming against the current, and known to take delight in upsetting established applecarts (I deliberately employ four clashing metaphors in a single sentence to emphasize the unreason involved.) The R.A. needn't be himself (or herself) a reader of the kind of literature we are out to save. We need his money, not his literary views. It is more important that he enjoy getting involved in conspiracies for their own sake, and that he not own any Simon & Schuster or Random House stock himself. For starters, does anyone in the room know Ted Turner?

(1994)

Versions of the Kingfish

1993 is the centenary of the birth of Huey Pierce Long, the Louisiana kingfish of the 1920s and 1930s and the subject of T. Harry Williams's prize-winning biography of 1969. Now we have another biography, *The Kingfish and His Realm* (1991), by one of Harry Williams's students, the late William Ivey Hair.

As governor of Louisiana and then as U.S. senator, Long achieved almost total political domination of his depression-ridden state. Making his appeal to the have-nots, riding roughshod over constitutional restraints, Long differed from other, garden-variety southern demagogues because he used his power to build roads, schools, and hospitals; and he forced the oil refineries and other interests that had hitherto controlled Louisiana's government to bear a fairer share of the tax burden. He also condoned and even encouraged widespread corruption, bribes, kickbacks and extortion, slimed and vilified his opponents, and made a farce of the customary checks and balances of representative government. He was busily engaged in moving onto the national scene when he was gunned down in the foyer of the skyscraper capitol he had built in Baton Rouge in 1935.

Harry Williams's biography won both a Pulitzer prize and a National Book Award, and was a best-seller. Why, one might wonder, did Professor Hair feel the need to produce yet another biography, especially after his mentor supposedly covered the subject so well? There is, after all, not a great deal more factual material extant than was available to Harry Williams—and, indeed, no small portion of Hair's documentation is drawn from the extensive interviews that Williams compiled in the course of writing his biography. When Williams was preparing his book in the late 1950s and the 1960s, there were hundreds of persons still alive who had been involved in Louisiana politics during Huey's time. By the time that Hair set out to write his book, the dramatis personae were almost all gone.

Let me say at once that Hair's new biography *is* justified, for the reason that it is his interpretation of Huey Long and what made him tick, and not Williams's, that comes closer to the actual kingfish.

Hair said this about Williams's biography of Long: "The book is richly detailed and skillfully blends narrative with analysis. Williams concedes that the kingfish loved power and eventually became obsessed with it, yet offers excuses for most of his actions. He credits Long with sincerity of purpose. In the opinion of this writer, Williams was overly sympathetic to Huey Long. But Professor Williams was a great scholar and teacher, and one of the things this writer, as a student at LSU, learned from him was that historians may honestly and respectfully disagree."

I knew Harry Williams fairly well, though he was not a close friend. He not only stomached disagreement but thrived on it. A midwesterner, he joined the Louisiana State University faculty in the early 1940s. Williams entered the profession of history as a Lincoln scholar, with *Lincoln and the Radicals* (1941); he then moved into the field of military history: his *Lincoln and His Generals* (1952) was widely read and enthusiastically reviewed. Adapting to his Louisiana surroundings, he then wrote an excellent biography of the Confederate general, Pierre Gustave Toutant Beauregard (1954).

I came to know him in the summer of 1957, when, although a literary scholar by profession, I taught two courses in southern history at L.S.U. Frank Vandiver, whose biography of Stonewall

Jackson, *Mighty Stonewall* (1956), had recently appeared, was also teaching there that summer; and, from the standpoint of military history, the two of us were strongly pro-Confederate in allegiance and given to refighting the war. Harry Williams, despite his work on Beauregard, was of the other persuasion. A great deal of off-duty debate went on. Vandiver and I repeatedly sought to gang up on Williams, but in wit, trenchant observation, and astute hyperbole he was more than a match for both of us.

The segregation crisis was going on in the South, and there was no disagreement among us about the right and wrong of that. Williams had a keen eye for absurdity of any kind, and the bluster of prosegregation southerners disgusted him. He said something once that delighted my wife. "All they can talk about is 'big buck niggers,' " he declared. "Weren't there ever any *little* buck niggers?"

Harry Williams was also, however, dismayed by the penchant of his fellow academic historians for taking pious stands, as if complex and difficult human passions and needs were not involved in what was going on. By nature and temperament an iconoclast, he delighted in puncturing the humorless solemnity with which so many academic types go about their work. In his later years this penchant became more and more a mannerism, and he tended to see himself as a beacon of practicality and common sense in a dense sea of scholarly abstraction. Perhaps because he had written military history for so long, and because many academic historians tended to disparage military history and its practitioners, Williams tended to play the role of gadfly. Yet no one could be more generous, more helpful to younger colleagues; those who knew him quickly recognized the kindliness and gentleness that lay behind the wit and iconoclasm.

Like most really good historians Williams was emotionally involved in his material. Unlike many he made no show of appearing dispassionate and scientifically objective in everyday discourse, though as a scholar he compiled his facts carefully and did not cavalierly arrange them to bear out his own predilections. He knew well that in writing history he was dealing with human beings caught in volatile emotional issues, not pasteboard figures in a scriptural parable; and he realized that the attitude of the historian can be more than a little involved in the interpretation of facts and the conclusions drawn from them.

A trained and careful historian, he was also an accomplished histrio: he liked to strike poses and dramatize issues. He tended to identify himself with his subjects. Writing about Lincoln, he saw things in Lincolnian terms. Once he got involved with Huey Long he became the unvarnished, practical-minded politico confronting the stuffed shirts.

I once secured three identical photos of Williams, and mounted them alongside one another. On the first I inked in a silk hat, a chin beard, and a bow tie; I greyed the hair of the middle photo, added a moustache, painted in gold shoulder epaulets, a military collar, and a gray jacket with a row of gold buttons; on the last I tousled the hair, opened the shirt collar and added a wide necktie with the slipknot halfway down. Under the first photo I wrote "With malice to none, with charity for all"; under the second, "Southrons, I have come to lead you in the defense of your liberties"; and under the third, "I'm gonna bust them dudes in the legislature with my bare hands," or something to that effect. I had it framed and shipped to him; he was delighted, and thereafter it graced his office wall.

By 1957, when I taught history at L.S.U., he had begun work on the Long biography, and he was full of the subject. Williams immersed himself in the Louisiana political scene of the 1920s and 1930s. He combed through newspaper files, examined masses of documents, legal and governmental records, took notes from exhaustive scrapbooks that had been maintained about the kingfish and his reign by libraries and individuals, and interviewed some three hundred persons who had either supported or opposed the kingfish, thereby creating a monumental oral history record for himself and future scholars to use.

It was a massive exercise in documentary research and oral history, and as Williams's zeal for his investigations became ever more ardent and his understanding of the milieu in which his subject lived and flourished expanded, he came more and more to see the Louisiana political situation through the kingfish's eyes. Writing about Huey Long, imaginatively and sympathetically he *became* Long.

I watched him in midseason form at a symposium held at Rice University under Frank Vandiver's aegis in 1963, at a time when he was engrossed in his research and his writing was well under way. The symposium papers were subsequently published as a book entitled *The Idea of the South: Pursuit of a Central Theme,* edited by Vandiver (1964). Williams's essay was "Trends in Southern Politics," and in many ways it is a précis of his forthcoming biography—and not only in its view of Huey Long's political role, but for what it reveals of his own attitude toward Long's career.

No small part of his address—rather more, I believe, than the published version would indicate—was devoted not to southern politics as such, but to scolding his fellow academics for their refusal to recognize the necessary impurity of the political process, which he said had much to do with the disrepute that the term *politician* had come to hold for most Americans.

"The professors have thought," Williams declared, "that the politicians should act much like themselves: debating issues with calm, balance, and scholarly restraint; presenting plans of doctrine, detail, and logic; acting, in short, like sweet philosophers. That politicians do not conform to these standards is obvious—and shocking to the detached campus observers, who fail to realize that they are upholding impossible standards. The politicians could not exist if they acted like professors."

Williams went on to declare that the "academic analysts are

responsible—along with an allied group—the moralists, the reformers, the 'good people'—for popularizing another unrealistic concept of politics, the doctrine of what might be called the double standard. It demands that politicians be more honest than anybody else, that, in fact, they be completely and consistently honest, making no compromises and no concessions but standing always on eternal principles." Politicians, he noted, "are constantly making deals and arrangements and concessions. This is disturbing to people who have been conditioned to believe that politics is a moral activity." The result was that the "average voter" was inclined to conclude that all politicians were crooks, and to develop a "cynicism that turns interest away from government and may be highly dangerous to the democratic system itself."

Williams then proceeded to point up the failure of southern, in particular Louisiana, politics over the decades to deal with the real needs of the mass of its people, and the resulting willingness to allow the race issue to override the dire need to do something about economic conditions. "Despite all the protests and the partial reforms, the salient fact about Southern life as the 1930s opened was poverty, grinding, abject poverty that afflicted most people of most races. In most Southern states the old ruling class still held the reins of government. It was 'government by goatee,' by gentlemen in frock coats and wide hats. It was stuffy and stale, and it was almost oblivious to the cravings and needs of ordinary people."

He went on from there to make the case for Huey, who unlike other southern demagogues *did* do something about poverty and want. He built good roads, expanded education, extended public-health facilities, and enlarged social services. The kingfish, he declared, was not content to marshal the support of the masses and then reach an accommodation with the ruling establishment; he realized that to secure his aims it was necessary to "destroy its base of power, its source of sustenance. A supreme power artist, he aimed to force the opposition into his organization on his terms and to control all branches of the state government, and he came close to succeeding."

The result, Williams declared, was that the practice of politics in Louisiana was forced to deal with the real issues: "Of all the mass leaders he was the only one who forced an element of realism into Southern politics. He made people think about the problems of their own day. We do not live in the Old South, he said, or in the Civil War or in Reconstruction. We live now and we can solve our problems now. . . . In Long's thinking the issues that mattered were those of economics and power. The issue of race that agitated so many politicians was to him an artificial and romantic question."

I remember talking with Harry Williams afterward, expressing my delight in his performance and in his analysis of the failure of southern politics, but telling him that I thought there had been too much rhetoric devoted to the sins of the historical fraternity: the economic, social and political problems of the South were, after all, scarcely ascribable to the shortcomings of professors of history.

What I perceive now is—and this is one of the reasons why Harry Williams was so fine a writer of history—that he was really engaged in arguing with himself. For he was deeply and emotionally involved in writing the biography of a man who had undeniably brought about desperately needed reforms in Louisiana society. Yet the man who had achieved this had not only gained the power to do it by rabble-rousing, name-calling, bribery, intimidation, payoffs, flagrant corruption, and a reckless disregard for the processes of law, fair play, and free speech, but he had been in love with personal power, craved it so desperately that he had been willing to do anything to acquire it, and had placed so high a premium on his capacity to wield it that he had virtually destroyed the ability of his constituency to restrain his actions or to remove him from office through orderly processes of democratic government.

Williams was writing a book about a man who had become a dictator. He had annihilated his opposition, all but eliminated its power to contest his rule through political processes. His regime had the right to select all electoral commissioners and pollwatchers for Democratic Party primary elections, which were the only elections that mattered—i.e., to count the votes. Local courts were forbidden by law to interfere with the removal of voter lists from registrars' offices, which meant that Long's appointed officials could decide in effect who was to be permitted to vote. Another law created a state printing board, appointed by him, to decide which newspapers in Louisiana would be given contracts to run the local legal advertising on which weekly newspapers in particular greatly depended for their existence; in effect he could now force the anti-Long press to choose between silence or financial ruin. And to back up his decrees he now had at his disposal a personal plainclothes police force known as the Bureau of Criminal Identification, the personnel of which were unknown to the public, empowered to make investigations and arrests and answerable only to Long's puppet governor—i.e., a secret police.

Can it really be said, as Williams contended, that the kingfish and his regime were subject at any moment to recall by the electorate? Long's opponents in Louisiana certainly thought not. So did not a few members of the U.S. Congress, for as William Ivey Hair notes in his biography, the speaker of the House of Representatives had appointed a seven-member committee to develop a congressional investigation into whether the state of Louisiana still had a republican form of government as specified in the U.S. Constitution.

Harry Williams was imaginatively drawn to Long. The talent for realpolitik that had enabled the kingfish to do what he had done for the people of Louisiana appealed to Williams's pragmatic attitudes and his impatience with high-sounding abstractions and holier-than-thou moralizing. Long's irreverence, his gift for savage but comic invective and the delight he took in puncturing pomposity and sham, his ability to cut through the nonessentials and the rhetorical façades and get at underlying issues, spoke directly to Williams's own iconoclasm and distaste for cant.

He wanted very much to believe that Huey Long, despite all his faults, was on the side of the angels, and I think his belaboring of his fellow historians for what he declared was their unwillingness to accept the fact that politics was necessarily an impure, frequently dirty profession was a way of assuaging any self-doubts he had about his choice of heroes.

Deep down Harry Williams was an idealist, who believed in heroes; his irreverence and iconoclasm were ways of concealing a deeply held faith in popular democracy and an admiration for dedicated, high-minded leadership. Robert B. Heilman, in a masterly review of Williams's *Huey Long*, relates a telling exchange that took place at a discussion group at L.S.U. in the early 1940s, in which Williams clashed with the refugee scholar and political philosopher Eric Voegelin: "Voegelin said something to the effect that, if this was indeed 'the century of the common man,' as it was often called, things were in a bad way. Williams bridled, since he tended to be rather an admirer of the 'common man.' Their difference became clear when someone asked the disputants whom they meant by the 'common man.' Williams said, 'Lincoln.' Voegelin said, 'Hitler.' "

Abraham Lincoln was a political pragmatist who combined a profound knowledge of recalcitrant human nature with a tenacious faith in democracy and freedom. And that is what Harry Williams very much wanted to believe was true of Huey Long. Yet Williams was forced to concede that the more power Long acquired, the more he desired, and that, during the final years of his hegemony, power itself became his dominant objective.

Not until late in Williams's massive biography does he come to terms with that realization. Long, he writes, "wanted to do good, but to accomplish that he had to have power. So he took power and then to do more good seized still more power, and finally the means and the end became so entwined in his mind that he could not distinguish between them, could not tell whether he wanted power as a method or for its own sake. He gave increasing attention to building his power structure, and as he built it, he did strange, ruthless, and cynical things."

Williams never gave up his belief that Long's intentions, no matter how he might have abused and confused them toward the end, were good, and that he genuinely and earnestly sought political power to better the condition of the plain people. The epilogue to his biography depicts Long as he lay dying, his sickroom crowded with politicians, and ends with what most of those present at his bedside remembered as Long's last words: "God, don't let me die. I have so much to do."

The difference between Harry Williams's and William Ivy Hair's interpretations of Huey Long is that Hair does not so believe. Hair's presentation of Long is of a man whose ruling motivation, from childhood on, was personal ambition: he craved the limelight, craved power, was ruthless in his quest for it, and would do anything to achieve it. Where Williams sees the idealist who is ultimately corrupted by power, Hair sees an unscrupulous megalomaniac. Long, he says, "led by compulsion instead of statesmanship because he was internally driven by a force he seemed unable to control. His brilliant and retentive mind took no time for reflection or intellectuality; he denied himself both restraint and breadth of vision. Huey focused his genius upon specific situations that could be aimed toward the only goal that truly mattered—the domination of everybody around him." For Hair "the conclusion is inescapable that everything he did in politics was for the purpose of augmenting his own power."

Williams's biography is far more exhaustive than Hair's, and goes into elaborate detail about incidents and events that Hair either omits or barely mentions—though it should be said that Hair offers a considerably broader picture of Louisiana's sorry state of race relations after the Civil War; and throughout he disabuses readers of the widely accepted notion that Huey Long was, unlike other southern spellbinders, hesitant about using race as an issue when it suited his needs.

Yet, although Williams's Huey Long is in every way a more fascinating and complex character than Hair's, and his biography is written with far more liveliness and verve, if one sets aside Williams's interpretations of Long's actions and focuses on the record itself, it is Hair's view of Huey Long that comes closer to fitting the facts.

Consider Long's behavior once he moved onto the national scene. When he realized that he was not going to be allowed to dominate the incoming Democratic administration, he lost no time in breaking with it. Within three days of Roosevelt's inauguration he was already publicly criticizing the new president, and thereafter he fought Roosevelt and the New Deal tooth and nail. Instead of cooperating with the programs to help ease the crippling burden of the Great Depression and use the resources of the national government to alleviate the nation's economic woes, he treated Roosevelt as a rival operator and did all he could to undermine public support for the New Deal, claiming that more radical legislation was needed. Using the floor of the U.S. Senate as a platform to publicize himself and his Share Our Wealth clubs, he taunted Roosevelt, ridiculed his administration, and schemed to set up a third political party.

The administration retaliated by denying him any say in the expenditure of federal relief funds in Louisiana, and from mid-1933 until Long's death in 1935 a state of open warfare existed between the kingfish and the New Deal. In 1935 Long fought against such key New Deal measures as the Wealth Tax Act, the Wagner Act setting up the National Labor Relations Board, the Works Progress Administration, and the Social Security Act, filibustering against the last until Roosevelt was forced to divert WPA and National Recovery Act funds to begin funding it. As far as Long was concerned, it was rule or ruin.

Roosevelt, no mean political tactician himself, was quick to recognize what the kingfish was up to. He sensed at once that behind Long's apparent concern for the toiling masses lay an ambition that would hesitate at nothing. "It's all very well for us to laugh at Huey," he remarked during the presidential campaign in 1932. "But actually we have to remember that he really is one of the two most dangerous men in the country"—the other being Douglas MacArthur.

Harry Williams's narrative, then, filled though it is with solid information about the Louisiana scene of the 1920s and 30s, written with great narrative skill and offering an unparalleled portrait of southern politics as practiced in Long's day, is not finally an accurate assessment of the Louisiana kingfish of historical record. Instead what Williams really wrote was a biography not of Huey Long, but of a fictional politician named Willie Stark.

In 1946 Robert Penn Warren published what is almost universally recognized as the finest of all American political novels, *All the King's Men*. He had taught English at Louisiana State University near the very end of Huey Long's career, but he always insisted that his novel, although it could never have been written had Long not existed, was not a fictionalized portrait of the kingfish but a work of fiction.

The central figure in Warren's novel, Willie Stark, is an earnest young man who finds himself running for governor, only to discover that he has been nudged into the race as a third candidate by one of the state's two dominant political factions in order to siphon off votes from the other's candidate. In his humiliation and rage he explodes into action, delivering a fiery speech that stirs and captures his rural audience as no other candidate has ever done. In a subsequent election he wins the governorship and proceeds to develop a program of good roads, better schools, and improved health services.

In so doing he takes on the state's power structure and becomes anathema to the old patrician families and industrial interests who have hitherto run the state for their own benefit, with little or no regard for the needs of the mass of its people.

Drawing on his ability to marshal the latent strength of the plain folk and to provide a voice for their hitherto-unarticulated aspirations, he creates a powerful political machine of his own, made up of divergent elements who come together out of both need and self-interest. His skill at identifying and blending those two factors, and his pragmatic grasp of the role of both, enables him to wield unparalleled power.

It is because along with his idealism he has a talent for gaining and wielding power that Willie Stark has been able to do these things. He is able to appeal to people on various levels, to be all things to all men. Willie accepts corruption as a necessary part of politics; he knows that his underlings make deals to keep his political machine functioning. He accepts the fact that politics is a dirty game, and that human motives are mixed: as a character says of him, " 'there's one principle he's grasped: you don't make omelettes without breaking eggs.' "

What brings Willie Stark down, however, is the abuse of power. He grows to be so comfortable with the power he has amassed that he comes to identify his own welfare with the public good and, on the theory that the end justifies the means, compromises his ideals to so great an extent that he becomes vulnerable.

There is no need here to rehearse the plot of Warren's novel, which involves complicated social and family relationships and rival claimants for Willie's patronage and affection. Suffice it to say that, after having built his regime on expediency, he is forced to confront the fact that he has compromised his ideals, whereupon he attempts to atone for his complicity by building a hospital that will be untouched by any tinge of expediency and corruption. In so doing he denies the working principles upon which the entire edifice of his political empire has been constructed, and thereby he touches off the chain of events that ends with his being shot and mortally wounded in the foyer of his state capitol building, under much the same circumstances as those that resulted in Huey Long's death.

The question of the relationship of Warren's novel to the career of Huey Long has been amply considered, and no purpose is served by rehearsing the arguments here. What is to the point is that in *All the King's Men* Warren produced the classic American political novel—so much so that most subsequent attempts to write political fiction have almost automatically been modeled upon it. He was able to bring his powers as a novelist to bear squarely upon the crucial problem of democracy—responsible leadership. If political power is derived from below—from the people, how can a leadership that addresses itself successfully to the masses and gains their support be made to exercise the power thus acquired for the ultimate benefit of those masses, rather than for selfish ends? The qualities that make for popular leadership—charisma, passionate involvement, and the ability to communicate that passion and dramatize issues to enlist the support and enthusiasm of voters—characteristically go along with a taste for power. The wish to provide needed leadership goes along with the wish to *be* the leader; and inevitably the temptation arises to identify the imperatives of the cause with the emotional needs of the leader of the cause, and to use the power derived from advocacy of the cause to gratify the private compulsions of the person entrusted with that power.

Warren's Willie Stark is just such a character. He sets out to do good, to offer the leadership that will enable the plain people to articulate their needs and compel the government of the state to address those needs; but from the start his wish to provide that leadership goes along with his desire to possess and exercise political power. He wants to be able to run the show—and ultimately his need to be the one who runs it becomes so important that he confuses the means with the ends, and compromises those ends beyond all hope of redemption. As he lies dying of his gunshot wounds, he tells Jack Burden that "It might have all been different, Jack." He repeats it twice: "You got to believe that." "All right," Jack replies. Then Willie adds, "And it might even have been different yet. . . . If it hadn't happened, it might—have been different—even yet." But there will be no further opportunity for it to be made good; what has happened has been done, and the bullets that will end Willie's story have been fired.

Thus Robert Penn Warren's Willie Stark. My point is that in its essential outlines the story that *All the King's Men* tells is equally the story that Harry Williams tells in his biography of Huey Long. In essence—in the shape and meaning assigned to his life and his career—Harry Williams's Huey Long *is* in effect Willie Stark. Nature, as Oscar Wilde insisted, has imitated art.

In the preface to his biography Williams makes the comparison himself:

> I also agree with what I understand to be the thesis of Robert Penn Warren in *All the King's Men:* that the politician who wishes to do good may have to do some evil to achieve his goal. This was the course that was forced on the hero of Warren's novel, Willie Stark, who was a politician much like Long. It was also the course that Long, faced with a relentless opposition, felt he had to follow. Stark was in the end possessed by the devil or the method and was destroyed. Long did not come to such a dramatic fate. But in striving to do good he was led on to grasp for more and more power, until finally he could not always distinguish between the method and the goal, the power and the good. His story is a reminder, if we need one, that a great politician may be a figure of tragedy.

Was that, however, really Huey Long? Not if we are to believe Hair's biography. And the man that Hair describes appears to me to come much closer to the real-life kingfish than does the man portrayed by Harry Williams—who seems to me to be modeled on a fictional character in a novel by Robert Penn Warren.

Robert B. Heilman, in his splendid essay-review, "Williams on Long," although finding himself in essential agreement with Williams's treatment of Long, stresses the literary nature of the biography. He notes that Williams is a "vivid teller of tall tales" who "says, in effect: let's enjoy the story, the comedy, the drama." Williams "uses fictional techniques—advance buildup of scene and situations, flashbacks, vivid imaging of physical appearances, suspense through unrevealed facts or outcome, intertwining plots, foreshadowing to increase tension, climax, 'continued in our next' (figuratively, that is)."

For Heilman, Williams is the "energetic, often-gay raconteur or impresario"; he has "a direct, flexible, sometimes-breezy style that avoids academic vices and embraces journalistic excellences— plainness, pace, variety, informality, unpretentiousness, and an occasional pinch of the slapdash and folksy." He concludes that "In the end, I think, Williams's book offers something like a literary experience: in the best sense, he presents a realistic fiction—that is, all the actions, all the behavior, all the relationships and battles that externalize the personality and the character of the hero. Our interest tends to shift from historic inquiry—what events actually took place?—to the human problem and the moral experience: what manner of man is this?"

Heilman believes that "instinctively Williams is less drawn to moralizing the fable than to dispensing delight." The mode of the biography, he declares, is that of "the most sophisticated comedy, a comedy where the danger is cynicism, the polar extreme of tragedy. And yet Huey's very diversity is the raw material of tragedy, which turns on the inner divisions that are the ultimate fact of human reality." But Williams, he says, although drawn to this view, does not finally come down on the side of tragedy; ultimately it is not Long's own qualities that bring him down. The qualities of tragedy within his makeup are there, and are revealed, but "he does not formally concede to them primacy in determination of the drama."

I am not convinced of this. Instead I believe that the qualities that make Williams's Huey Long into a figure of literary tragedy rather than political history are decisively developed. They lie in what

Williams as author and interpreter has *added* to the historical documentation. And this is, the overall depiction of Long as a figure who wished to do good, who sought power in order to do it, who in order to overcome the entrenched opposition that barred him from doing good was forced to seek ever more power, until ultimately he could no longer distinguish between "the method and the goal, the power and the good."

Such is the Huey Long Legend. But in actuality Long was hardly a thwarted idealist and reformer. Instead he was a politico who at all times craved power, wished to dominate, and whose actions were determined primarily by whatever was calculated to gain power. That all things considered he would have liked to further the well-being of the plain people—and certainly he did that—is no doubt true; but to see the wish to aid and elevate his fellow man as a principal or even an important motivation *at any time in his career* is to distort what Huey Long was all about. From the outset what he wanted, yearned for, and set out to win was absolute political domination.

He wanted to *rule;* he intended to crush anyone who sought to interfere with his rule; he took a savage delight not merely in defeating his political opponents but in humiliating them. His motto was "every man a king," but in his eyes there could be only one king, and he was going to be it. He intended to be governor of Louisiana and then president of the United States, and he was willing to say and do whatever it took to achieve those aims.

What Harry Williams did was to buy the Long Legend lock, stock, and barrel; the protagonist that emerges from his zestfully told biography is what he would have wanted the kingfish to be. He wanted to believe that this man of the people had acted out of the same idealism and faith in the democratic process that he, Harry Williams, brought to everything he did; that Long's callousness and disrespect for law were, like his own iconoclasm and irreverence, no more than a mask for generosity and the wish to help others; that Long's willingness to run roughshod over the tenets of decency and fair play and to countenance corruption, blackmail, and character assassination were only a game, and signified no more than the pragmatism that as a historian Harry Williams liked to apply to his own evaluations of human behavior. In short he wanted Huey Long to be what Harry Williams would have been under the same circumstances, which is to say something close to Willie Stark.

An interesting sentence in Williams's biography reveals his own thesis. He is describing an incident in 1934 in which Long was engaged in ramrodding a series of measures through the Louisiana legislature, including one that called for the naming of additional state-appointed members to various administrative boards in New Orleans. It was part of his policy of breaking the back of the New Orleans political machine by denying it control over the city's government.

Asked about his motives in adding the new members, Williams says, Long grinned and said that his own organization had to have more jobs at its disposal in the city. Then, noting that Long's apparent frankness in explaining his intentions was only superficial, Williams deposes as follows: "As he sometimes did, *he ascribed to himself lower motives than he actually had*" (italics mine). He goes on to say that the additional jobs were not merely needed for patronage or even to give Long more power as such, but to permit the kingfish to push through his "great plan" for the betterment of the state's economy—so that in turn it would serve as a pattern for what he would do when elected president.

Surely it is not the Huey Long of historical record, but the Long of Harry Williams's imagination, who is pretending that his motives for packing administrative boards with his own appointees were more crass and self-serving than was actually the case. That Harry Williams would be capable of deprecating his own idealism is quite believable; but that Huey Long would ever think to do so was most unlikely.

Williams's dazzling and moving portrait, then, is of a Louisiana kingfish not as he ever was but as his biographer would have wanted him to be. Filled with life and color, enthralling in its descriptions of politics and government in Louisiana during the Long years, enormously instructive in its depiction of the way that a political machine functions and of the impact that a powerful, charismatic individual can have on a community, Harry Williams's Huey Long is nonetheless importantly shaped by the author's creative imagination—a product of the historian as artist.

Let no one, however, thereby dismiss it as unworthy of the closest attention by anyone wishing to understand its historical subject. For what important work of history is not, in important respects, likewise the product of creative interpretation, and its judgments subject to its author's hopes and fears rather than restricted to coldly dispassionate analysis? One need only consider the variety of historical interpretations, complementary and contradictory, of the causes of the American Civil War, or of the nature of Reconstruction, to realize that not only do historians differ in their interpretations of which facts are and are not significant, but that the same sets of facts can produce quite different interpretations—interpretations that evolve, in part at least, from the interpreter's imaginative and emotional engagement with the material.

Indeed, in no unimportant sense, Williams's biography of Long is only the more useful because its author's interpretative bias is so very evident; for because it deals with such highly volatile and still controversial subjects, the reader can readily recognize where the factual presentation leaves off and the author's interpretation takes over. One is able to use Williams's matchless accumulation of material, draw upon his understanding of how the art of politics works, while yet identifying what is factual and what is Williams's interpretative thesis. Had Williams been less emotionally involved in his subject, had the enthusiasm and passion with which he went about writing his book been less overt, this would have been considerably more difficult to do.

It is important to understand, too, that the same passion and enthusiasm that led Harry Williams to model a picture of Huey Long which answered to his own needs and hopes are responsible for the zeal and thoroughness with which he went about compiling his factual material, and which made it possible for another historian such as William Ivey Hair to draw upon that material in order to arrive at a significantly different view of what the Louisiana kingfish was and meant. Reading Williams's biography we are able to separate the Williams in it from the Long; but we must also recognize that the data, the imposing historical records, are equally Williams. It is because Harry Williams saw Huey Long as he did, and therefore was impelled to write his biography, that the wealth of material that he uncovered is now on record instead of being lost.

We are fortunate, therefore, that this young midwestern-born historian of Abraham Lincoln ended up in Louisiana and was drawn to the study of that state's most charismatic and colorful politico. And we are fortunate, too, that he read *All the King's Men*.

(1993)

Friends and Occasions

The Gathering of the Fugitives:
A Recollection

I have a friend who says that the age of the printed book is over.
He says he's already given it a name—he says the Gutenberg period
is finished. [laughter] *Television is taking over. On the other hand,*
if he is right, and there is perhaps a little core of truth in what he is
saying . . .
                                    —Cleanth Brooks, *Fugitives' Reunion*

On May 3–5, 1956, in the city of Nashville, Tennessee, there took place a gathering that, if ever anybody writes a history of the practice of poetry in the South, ought to rate a page or two for its symbolic value alone. When I think back on its significance at the time, and also on what has happened to its participants since then, I marvel at—to echo the title of a volume of poems by one of those present—the noise that time makes.

During the early and mid-1920s, a group of young men in and about Vanderbilt University had published a little poetry magazine that cut a notable figure in the literary life of the nation. The magazine was called *The Fugitive,* and they became known as the Nashville Fugitives. What made the magazine and the group remarkable was that no less than four of the Fugitives and their close associates—John Crowe Ransom, Allen Tate, Robert Penn Warren, and Cleanth Brooks—became internationally renowned men of letters, while at least three others—Donald Davidson, Andrew Lytle, and, in a different way, Merrill Moore—came to possess distinctive reputations on the American literary scene.

These and the other Fugitives had almost all been students at Vanderbilt University, and several had taught there. By the time of the 1956 conclave, however, only Donald Davidson was still affiliated with the university. Moreover, during the three decades after *The Fugitive* suspended publication in 1925, Vanderbilt as an institution had shown almost no interest at all in the Fugitives.

There were reasons for this lack of proprietary pride. For one thing, during the late 1920s and early 1930s several of the members of the group had been the moving spirits behind the enterprise known as Agrarianism. They had published a book, *I'll Take My Stand: The South and the Agrarian Tradition* (1930), which questioned the South's belief in progress and urged the region to repudiate industrialization and hold fast to its old ways. This had not been popular with the university's administration, in particular its chancellor-czar, James H. Kirkland, nor was it of great help in raising endowment either from Tennessee industrialists or northeastern foundation executives. Moreover, as the issue of racial integration arose in the 1950s, Donald Davidson, the only ex-Fugitive still at Vanderbilt, took an increasingly outspoken pro-segregation position, which understandably embarrassed the university.

But it was not just that. The leading Fugitives and their magazine were practitioners and advocates of the poetry of modernism, and outspoken critical foes of the old mode of Victorian ideality. The longtime head of the Vanderbilt English department, Edwin Mims, was by contrast a devotee of Sidney Lanier, a reciter of Tennyson's "Ulysses," and and a purveyor of inspirational uplift in classrooms. His book *The Advancing South* (1926) represented almost everything that the Fugitives abominated about both the nature of society and the study of literature. A New South liberal, Eddie Mims ran the Vanderbilt English department like a private game preserve. There was much ill will between him and the leading Fugitives. In the 1920s, although he gave Ransom and Davidson teaching jobs, he had done nothing to encourage their magazine. In the mid-1930s he would not make the moderate concessions necessary to keep Ransom from moving to Kenyon College. In 1934, in an act of consummate academic stupidity, he let Red Warren go as instructor. Mims and Tate had clashed while the latter was still an undergraduate in the early 1920s; Tate's youthful arrogance punctured Mims's smugness and pomposity, and ever afterward they detested each other. Mims even wrote around to try to keep Tate from getting jobs.

The basic trouble between Mims and the Fugitives was generational; it was the Nineteenth Century versus the Twentieth, "The Song of the Chattahoochee" versus "The Waste Land." What it amounted to was that, as so often happens, when the distinction that Mims and Kirkland had sought from their English faculty materialized, it went unrecognized by them, and the little group of poets who had brought to Vanderbilt University almost the only national and international intellectual renown it had ever enjoyed were resented and ignored.

By the early 1950s, however, Kirkland was dead, Mims out of office, and the New South Victorians all but extinct. It could no longer be pretended that the leading Fugitives and their student and friend Cleanth Brooks were mere ephemeral modernists—not when they were known and quoted on several continents. It began to sink in that these people had become important literary figures. To honor such distinguished alumni, therefore, would be only meet and proper.

It so happened that Randall Stewart, Vanderbilt alumnus, Hawthorne scholar, and professor of English at Brown University, had decided in 1954 to return to his alma mater as chairman of the English department. It also happened that the present writer had taken a position as executive secretary of the newly formed American Studies Association in Philadelphia, with the responsibility of helping to set up regional associations. One of the regional groups involved was New England, and in the process I met Randall.

He was soon to go home to Tennessee. For my part, as traveling academic Rotarian I felt like a homeless wanderer, and nobody at the University of Pennsylvania, where I was based, had the slightest interest in southern literature. Between us we came up with the idea that I would use my position with the A.S.A. to try to get a foundation grant to stage a first-ever reunion of the Fugitives at Vanderbilt. I approached the Rockefeller Foundation, the head money-dispenser of which was a man named John Marshall, and succeeded in extracting $4,000 for Randall to use. We'd have gotten more, but, as I learned in later years, Marshall's guru in matters of the belles lettres was Richard P. Blackmur, who was at loggerheads with Allen Tate, and Blackmur apparently encouraged Marshall to keep the grant to the minimum.

With the $4,000 to help defray costs, Randall persuaded the now-receptive Vanderbilt authorities to stage a full-fledged three-day conclave, featuring public papers and poetry readings and closed sessions discussing what the Fugitive activity had been all about, the proceedings to be taped and transcribed, and a posh dinner banquet at the Belle Meade Country Club to be presided over by none other than the chairman of the Vanderbilt board of trust, Harold Vanderbilt himself, financial tycoon and America's Cup yachtsman.

What Randall soon found out was the extent to which the leading Fugitives still very much resented the university's failure, up until then, to give them the time of day. Even so, the fact that, however belatedly, Vanderbilt did now desire to pay the group homage meant a tremendous lot to all of them. That was a revelation to me, for I thought of them as figures of nationwide and even international fame, upon whom large honors had been heaped, and didn't then understand that humiliations experienced when young are never forgotten nor wholly forgiven.

To appreciate the impact of the Fugitives' Reunion, one must grasp the contemporary literary situation. By the 1950s the New Criticism had successfully entered the academy and was forcing even the most benighted pedants to read the actual words used in poems, instead of merely annotating historical, biographical, and philosophical contexts. The facile Marxism of the Depression years had been discredited. Existentialism and High Church theology were in vogue. T. S. Eliot was at the height of his influence; Ezra Pound was still incarcerated in St. Elizabeth's mental hospital. Except for a few Beat poets out on the West Coast, nobody much was engaged in literary parent-slaying. William Faulkner was coming into his own, and, on the stage, Tennessee Williams. The civil rights movement still lay ahead, so southern authors hadn't been made suspect in New York City. Eisenhower was consul, the Korean police action was over, and we were not yet involved in Viet Nam. The Old Left was dead; the New Left, unawakened. Structuralism, deconstruction, etc., were unheard of this side of Paris. Textual bibliography as a secular faith was distinctly small potatoes.

All was quiet, that is, on the Western Front, or so it appeared to be. It was a time when English professors, or a great many of them, still remembered the physical and spiritual indignities of military service during World War II well enough to remain content, for a while longer at least, with the privilege of reading and teaching literary works as stories and poems, without feeling it necessary to seek ideological justification for what they did.

It is easy to look back upon this period with nostalgia. I don't happen to do so, myself. But it is true that, in the realm of literature at least, the ideologues hadn't taken over, and the television tube hadn't yet importantly undermined the practice of intelligent reading for pleasure. In the quotation that prefaces this essay, note the bracketed word [*laughter*]; what Brooks said Marshall McLuhan was saying seemed comically ridiculous in 1956. Poetry—good poetry, serious poetry—was still being regularly published, if seldom at a profit, by all the major publishing houses; think of that! The mergers and conglomerates hadn't converted the trade book industry into sex and how-to-do-it purveyors, and the publishers of drugstore paperbacks didn't tell the publishers of clothbound fiction which titles they could print.

Now if this was approximately the way things were, then consider the literary prestige of those one-time Fugitives who were belatedly being brought back onto the Vanderbilt campus to be honored. Here were the leading, most influential of the New Critics—Ransom, whose *Kenyon Review* had for fifteen years been the central organ of the movement; Tate, whose essays were among its most powerful statements; Brooks and Warren, whose *Understanding Poetry* was its chief pedagogical manual. Brooks's *The Well-Wrought Urn* was greatly influential. As a poet, Warren was only beginning to approach his major mode, but *All the King's Men* and *World Enough and Time* were among the most widely read fiction in the land (the latter has totally receded, but the former still holds its place after a half-century.) No textbook anthology of verse could possibly neglect to include sizeable chunks of Ransom's and Tate's poetry and hope to be widely adopted.

Had any university, had any community elsewhere in the country turned out so remarkable a working group of distinguished authors? Harvard had more influential writers, to be sure, but they weren't a group; they hadn't met together, studied and taught together, constituted themselves a movement. Neither had the Chicago Poets of the early 1910s. Morphologically, the nearest thing to them seemed to be the Transcendentalists of pre–Civil War New England (whose poetics, ethics, and politics they detested), or the Irish of the early twentieth century (whom they admired greatly.)

In any event, to Vanderbilt they came, for three days of celebration and disputation. In addition to those who had become distinguished professional literary men—Ransom, Tate, Warren, Davidson, Lytle—there were others who had followed more remunerative professions. Merrill Moore, who had published a book of sonnets, *The Noise that Time Makes* (1929), had become a Boston psychiatrist and a compulsive writer of sonnets; indeed, he had written more than 50,000 such. He scrawled them down and never revised, even keeping a clipboard on the steering wheel of his car and composing between traffic lights. William Yandell Elliott was professor of government and director of the summer session at Harvard University; he had written assorted books on politics, was big on political theory, was a member of the National Security Council, and, had Richard Nixon defeated John F. Kennedy for president in 1960, would probably have been appointed National Security Adviser. Alec Brock Stevenson, Alfred Starr, and Jesse Wills were Nashville businessmen. Sidney Mttron Hirsch—but of him more later.

Those were the surviving Fugitives. Other persons were also part of the proceedings. Brooks was not technically a Fugitive, but as critic was indissolubly linked with the group. Richmond Croom Beatty was professor of English at Vanderbilt. Dorothy Bethurum, a medievalist, had been at Vanderbilt in the early 1920s, and was professor of English at Connecticut College for Women. Frank L. Owsley was a distinguished southern historian who had taught at Vanderbilt during the 1920s, taken part in *I'll Take My Stand,* and was then at the University of Alabama. Willard Thorp was professor of English at Princeton, a well-known American literature scholar, and the recent editor of an anthology, *A Southern Reader.* William Cobb, a Vanderbilt student in the early 1920s, was the Rockefeller Foundation's editor of publications. And Randall Stewart was on hand for all sessions.

There were also three younger participants in the discussions. Louise Cowan had a book coming out on the Fugitives. Robert D. Jacobs and I were co-editors of *Southern Renascence: The Literature of the Modern South* (1953). I had left the American Studies Association and was temporarily (and, as was swiftly becoming evident to me, uncomfortably) out of the academic world as associate editor of the afternoon newspaper in Richmond, Virginia. At thirty-two, I was the youngest one present.

The Reunion consisted of several public sessions, including banquets and a poetry reading, and four private sessions. There was a certain amount of uneasy political tension having to do with Donald Davidson's passionate involvement with the Tennessee Federation for Constitutional Government, formed to combat the *Brown v. Board of Education* decision of the U.S. Supreme Court two years earlier, and the "alien" political positions, as Davidson saw it, of William Yandell Elliott and Merrill Moore in particular. (John Ransom was also suspect.) The other participants also had political views, sometimes quite strongly held, but they were able to stick to the subject at hand. Not so the embattled Davidson, who at one point publicly challenged Elliott to a constitutional debate to be held on the steps of any county courthouse in Tennessee.

The avowed intention of the closed discussion sessions—which is to say, the justification advanced to the Rockefeller Foundation in order for the grant to be awarded—was to try to get at some of the cultural, historical, and creative dynamics that had produced the Fugitives as a literary group. The leading Fugitives, of course, all expressed their skepticism. And if one looks in the published transcript (1959) of the closed discussions—*Fugitives' Reunion: Conversations at Vanderbilt, May 3–5, 1956*, edited by Rob Roy Purdy—for any considered explanation for the emergence of the group, it will not be found. Perhaps the closest thing to an answer was offered by a non-participant in the discussions, Chancellor Harvie Branscomb of Vanderbilt, at the dinner at the Belle Meade Country Club. "You were young, brilliant, and restless," he told the group; "and I take it the University added considerably to your spiritual unrest and discontent, and maybe that was its contribution to the Fugitive movement."

It was indeed. For the Vanderbilt of the 1910s and 1920s was, more so than any other college or university south of the Ohio and

Potomac Rivers, intellectually a cosmopolitan place, with a distinguished faculty, many of whom came from the great world outside of the South. It had money—as no other southern institution did until Duke emerged from Trinity College in 1924. Methodist by endowment, it had nonetheless thrown off the control of the church bishops, and, like a magnet, it drew its student body from the brightest and most ambitious youths of the Upper South, many of them Methodists and not a few the sons of preachers, along with numerous outlanders.

Culturally it was a volatile mix, and needed only a catalyst, or catalysts, to set it ablaze. Or to use another metaphor, the cultural and spiritual inheritors of the economically threadbare tradition-bound orthodoxy of the defeated nineteenth-century South were engaged in coming into violent intellectual collision with the vanguard of twentieth century Western thought, belief, and culture.

That sort of thing was not discussed during the sessions, yet it was there. More than that, it was reenacted before the eyes of those watching. For once the Fugitives began arguing about poetry, it made no difference that thirty years had elapsed since their little magazine, *The Fugitive,* had ceased publication and the group had ceased to meet. The discussions quickly reproduced some of the tensions that had once startled the young Fugitives into becoming good poets.

At the first discussion session a dispute developed about why none of the Fugitives had ever written an epic poem. On the face of it, this was a silly enough matter, the epic having properly died a natural death several hundred years earlier. But what the argument was really about was the poetry of modernism, and the line of allegiance was between those who had become professional men of letters and those who hadn't.

The most often-heard voice throughout was that of William Yandell Elliott, a well-read political scientist enthralled with his own brand of wisdom. He was abetted by Merrill Moore and Alfred Starr. Elliott had never written poetry of any consequence, nor had Starr.

Merrill Moore's reputation was for quantity, not quality—a psychiatrist, as noted earlier, he cranked out hordes of sonnets.

Needless to say, *all* of the Fugitives had failed to write epics, but only *some* had failed to write important lyric poetry; as Warren remarked when asked about his recently completed *Brother to Dragons*, "It never crossed my mind I was trying to write an epic, I'll say that." But here was this comical attempt by men who, whatever their distinction in other fields, were at best mediocrities as poets, to tell several of the more important poets of their time what the latter should have written but hadn't.

It was obvious to those who looked on that what the non-pros really wanted was a poetry of ideas, uplift—in short, a return to the kind of verse that could attract a wide popular audience. What they resented was what they considered to be the hyperintellectuality, verbal complexity, and allusiveness of twentieth-century verse. Here, then, obliquely on display, was one of the tensions that had most invigorated the Fugitive poets during their formative time—the practice and promulgation of the poetry of modernism.

Modern, or as it is known today, modernist, poetry is under frequent attack as being elitist, escapist, anti–Third World, covertly Anglican, reactionary, etc. But in the 1910s and 1920s it constituted, for poets who were serious about their craft, the only way to go. For poetry to reclaim its role as an important mode of human utterance, it was necessary for it to purge itself of the empty abstraction, high-sounding rhetoric, and artificial poetic diction of late Victorian ideality, which prevented it from dealing with the poet's own experience. ("Chicago sitteth at the northwest gates," William Vaughn Moody declared in a poem in the 1890s.) The alternative was dilettantism and superficiality.

The flaccid language needed to be reinvigorated and the evasive platitudes discarded; the poet, as T. S. Eliot insisted, must force the intellectual and emotional complexity of contemporary experience into the poem, at the risk of ignoring a general middle-class audience. (For every person who read "The Waste Land," a hundred read *John Brown's Body*.) The future professionals in the Fugitives had accepted that, and were willing to pay the price. The others, who had been unwilling to make poetry into a central activity in their lives, had felt themselves increasingly excluded from the discourse as the 1920s went on, and they argued against the direction that verse was taking. Thirty years later, at the Reunion, they were still doing so.

The role that Donald Davidson played in the debate was revelatory. For readers who do not remember him—he was a dear friend of mine—and what he stood for, some explanation will be necessary. Allen Tate and others thought him the most technically gifted of the Fugitives. By the later 1920s, however, after Tate had departed Nashville and concurrent with his own whole-souled and literal involvement with Agrarianism, Davidson had moved into a subject matter drawn from southern and Tennessee history, and his poetry became hortatory and even polemical. As the only important Fugitive who stayed on at Vanderbilt—in his introductory remarks he likened himself to the boy who stood on the burning deck, whence all but him had fled—he developed an intense antipathy toward modernism, cosmopolitanism, industrialism, the urban Northeast, and political and social liberalism, all of which he saw as a single cultural entity. In effect he grew to oppose most of the major intellectual and social currents of his time, and to view the older, agricultural South as a lost elysium. As might be expected, the desegregation court decisions of the 1950s greatly exercised him.

Davidson had always tended to distrust literature as a self-sufficient mode; in his essay in *I'll Take My Stand* (1930) he had declared that it was time for the poet to leave his literary perch and function as a citizen in order to make the world safe for poetry—i.e., to place poetry in the service of ideology. By the mid-1950s he had developed a theory of poetry that stressed its lyric folk origins and deprecated its conversion into a printed medium with, as he saw it, its resulting irony, intellectualism, and (in a very different context than its use nowadays) elitism.

He had opened the first evening's public session with an address to that effect, declaring that "A poetry that puts itself in a position not to be recited, not to be sung, hardly ever to be read aloud from the page where it stands, almost never to be memorized, is nearing the danger age of absurdity."* His remarks had touched off the argument about the epic the next morning; Tate had declared in reply that "we haven't got a choice between literary poetry, as you describe it, and this pure Pierian spring, folk literature. It's a choice between literary poetry or none at all: the canned poetry, manufactured for a super-bourgeois society." Elliott thereupon brought up the failure, as he saw it, of the Fugitives to produce an epic—i.e., to write poetry about larger-than-life heroes and heroines, grounded in a generally accepted social *mythos,* for a general audience, which is to say, popular poetry.

Once Elliott and his allies began implicitly to attack the Fugitives for not having developed a popular poetry, however, Donald Davidson ceased slating the poetry of modernism for failing to be what it couldn't be, and joined Tate, Ransom, Warren, and Brooks in defending its literary integrity against the demand that it perform the function of a Platonic absolute. When that happened, one could see what Davidson had lost by the departure of his fellow Fugitive poets, in particular Allen Tate. Without the stimulus and encouragement of the others, he had moved into an intellectual and emotional position whereby he stopped using his poetry to examine his experience, and began employing it to defend and to expound previously determined conclusions. His poetry did not recreate his experience in language so much as invoke already-held patriotic

---

*Davidson's statement, like those of Chancellor Branscomb cited earlier, does not appear in Fugitives' Reunion. It is drawn from the transcribed proceedings from which the book was produced.

emotions; it became didactic. The modern world became ever more menacing to him; his imagination and his energy were expended in a vain attempt to fend off the twentieth century. This generous, warm-hearted, loyal, richly creative man, with his abundant capacity for friendship, ended up building a wall between himself and his private experience that the language of poetry could not scale.

On the afternoon of the second day of the Reunion, another striking reenactment took place. To understand what this involved, some explanation is necessary. When the nucleus of the group that eventually became the Fugitives first began convening in 1914–1915, it was principally to discuss philosophy, not poetry. They—Davidson, Ransom, Elliott, several others—met at the home of Mr. and Mrs. James Frank, and the discussions, which were informal, were led by Mrs. Frank's brother-in-law, Sidney Mttron Hirsch.

Then in his early thirties, Hirsch was a full-fledged mystic, versed in Rosicrucianism, Oriental philosophies, numerology, etymology, astrology, Hebraic lore, Buddhism, Taoism, and the like. He had been heavyweight boxing champion of the U.S. Navy's Pacific fleet, served as a model for Rodin, been friends with Gertrude Stein, George Russell (AE), Edwin Arlington Robinson, and the sculptor Gertrude Vanderbilt Whitney. One of his plays, *The Passion Play of Washington Square,* was performed on the vaudeville circuit, and in 1913 his Greek pageant, *The Fire Regained,* was produced in Nashville with a cast of 600, and including chariot races, 300 sheep, and 1,000 pigeons. A large, powerful man, he had developed an obscure back injury which somehow prevented his working for a living.

It was Hirsch who in 1921 proposed that the group, which by then had focussed its interests on poetry, publish a magazine, and its name was drawn from one of Hirsch's mystical poems, "The Fugitive Blacksmith." When the Reunion opened he was not present but remained at home, sulking in his tent, until Merrill Moore went over and fetched him. Once there, he tended to dominate the proceedings, using his Socratic method to elucidate his mystical theory whereby poets and other superior seers were possessed of certain truths denied to the multitude and which were handed down across the ages in the form of myths. Accompanying this was a strange kind of etymology, in which certain key words in various languages evoked mysterious symbolic truths.

At the session before Sidney Hirsch's appearance, Elliott said of him that "You must feel his power to understand his part in our beginnings." This is precisely what took place that afternoon. Most of what Hirsch said was nonsensical, but as a demonstration of his early role it was a decided success. One could indeed perceive what the impact of his personality and the kind of esoteric, non-rational, non-logical thought and lore he professed must have been on a group of extremely bright, imaginative young men who had been reared in the turn-of-the-century rural South and sent off to Nashville for a university education.

It must be remembered that the leading Fugitives were from small towns in Tennessee and Kentucky. By their youthful standards, Nashville was large, cosmopolitan, eclectic. Not only Hirsch and the several other Southern urban Jews who were part of the group, but Vanderbilt University itself, with its highly educated professorate and varied student body, constituted for these young men an abrupt and exciting contrast, intellectually, socially, physically, with what they'd known and been taught.

Sidney Hirsch did not reappear at later Reunion sessions, which was just as well, for while he was present the other Fugitives all tended to pull their punches, and other than the example of his presence he had nothing to contribute to most of what was being discussed. But the fact, and the force, of his personality upon that one occasion was, in eccentrically dramatic fashion, very evident. In Donald Davidson's words, "his constant probings into mythologies and religions brought results that astounded some of us, even when we argued against him. Most of all, his declaration of the high eminence of poetry somehow elevated into an almost priestly rite the consideration of the most juvenile and humble of our verses." (*Southern Writers in the Modern World*)

Since their Vanderbilt days they had traveled far and wide. Ransom, Brooks, Warren, and Elliott were Rhodes scholars; during the conference Elliott constantly alluded to his status as Balliol man. Ransom and Davidson had served overseas during the First World War. To coin a phrase, Nashville had served as their launching pad into the twentieth-century intellectual and artistic cosmos. As Chancellor Branscomb said, being there at Vanderbilt had indeed "added considerably" to the young Fugitives' "spiritual unrest and discontent," and as poets and literary men they had striven to give the order and form of language to the confusion and incongruity of their experience. Red Warren picked up on Branscomb's remark at the public reading later that evening. "Versifying," he remarked, "should be the process of converting human irritation into divine discontent," and, he added, "Vanderbilt had a gift in that direction, whatever the results." What the 1956 Reunion helped to show were the particular circumstances under which it happened.

Relatively little was said during the proceedings about the impact on the group of the poetry of modernism, as it was being written by Eliot, Pound, the later Yeats, and others. On other occasions, however, Ransom and Davidson made it clear that the young Allen Tate, being precociously read in the French symbolists and conversant with modern poetry, did much to perform that service. Coming from Kentucky, with no close connections among the Tennessee Methodist families from which most of the Fugitives arose, Tate introduced into their deliberations a boldness of metaphor and a literary sophistication that was a crucial addition to their experience. There was an important sense in which Tate did not belong to the stable, traditional, rural community from which the Fugitives arose, and he brought to their affairs, particularly those involving Agrarianism, the zeal of the convert. So, if the volatile literary mix that existed in Nashville in the early 1920s required a catalyst or catalysts to cause it to explode, then beyond doubt Allen Tate helped to provide it.

At the time the Fugitives' Reunion was held—1956, some forty years ago—the group appeared, except for Merrill Moore's compulsive sonneteering, to have given up the writing of poetry. Ransom, next to Hirsch the oldest, later produced bizarre revisions of some of his better poems, which his publishers wisely insisted upon adding to rather than substituting for the earlier versions. He wrote a little more criticism, but even though he lived until 1974, essentially his literary career was over.

Davidson experienced a new spurt of poetic activity in the 1950s and 1960s, which however attracted little critical attention; stylistically and in attitude his poems, carefully constructed and often beautifully wrought, were by then out of critical fashion. He died in 1968. Tate wrote some more criticism, but no more poetry; he died in 1979 at the age of eighty. His later years were embittered by the erosion of his influence in the national literary firmament. In his heyday he had exercised formidable power in the awarding of fellowships, prizes, appointments, etc., and in what got published in magazines and books. With the rise of the New Left, his poetics and his politics alike became anathema to the young and the militant. He married a fourth time, fathered children in his seventies, quarreled with old friends, and went out into that good night in most ungentle fashion. One literary generation's incendiary becomes the next's establishment figure; it was a sad end for a good poet and busy literary politico who had helped so many poets do so many good things.

Andrew Lytle published another novel, a delightful memoir, and several books of criticism, edited the *Sewanee Review* with distinction, and as of this writing [1994], is still drinking good whiskey at the age of ninety-one. Merrill Moore died within a year of the Reunion, in 1957; what happened to the "sonnetorium" he built to house his 50,000+ sonnets, I have no idea.

Cleanth Brooks took on a whole new critical lease on life by turning to the criticism of prose fiction, writing what remains the most solid and influential of readings of the work of William Faulkner, and continuing thereafter to produce all manner of criticism; he is now eighty-five and working with undiminished vigor. Changing critical fashions have made him, as the war horse of the New Criticism, the target for every ambitious structuralist, deconstructionist, or whatever desiring to commit critical parricide, but he goes right on about his business of reading poems and stories as poems and stories.

The Fugitive poet whose day was emphatically not yet done in 1956 was Robert Penn Warren. At the opening public session he made a remark that nowadays reads very quaintly: "I suppose we all hope to write some more [poetry] some day. I haven't written any verse for a year and a half. I suppose I am here under false pretenses. . . . I've been trying to practice the simpler art of writing prose lately." In the verse drama he had recently published, however, *Brother to Dragons* (1953), a voice designated as "R.P.W." functions as a device for arguing with Thomas Jefferson about the meaning of what happens. Apparently the discovery of that first-person perspective had the result of liberating Red Warren's muse, for beginning with *Promises: Poems 1954–1956* (1957) he produced book after book of poems—long poems, short poems, poems in sequence, interconnected poems, just about every kind of poem.

To do this, it was necessary for him to break with the earlier poetics of the Fugitives, which had enabled Ransom and Tate to do their best work, and to move into a more colloquial, personal, less Literary style, which provided him with a freedom that, for all the considerable merits of his earlier poems, had been hitherto absent in his verse. Where Tate's poetry had been confessional, and Ransom's an ironic marshaling of contrarieties, Warren's mature verse was ruminative, autobiographical, and meditative, with an overt, active role for the persona. Uneven in quality—neither in poetry nor prose was Warren the kind of writer who avoided risks—it is often breathtaking in its lyrical brilliance.

Of all the Fugitive poets, then, Warren was the only one whose most important verse was written after the 1956 Reunion. Could any of those present in Nashville on that occasion have predicted that three decades later Red would still be publishing new poem after poem, the latest fruits of an active literary career which stretched more than six decades beyond the Fugitive years of the early 1920s? When he died in 1989, he left behind him a body of work, in poetry, fiction, drama, and nonfiction, such as few important American writers have ever compiled.

It should be no cause for surprise that Time has not dealt gently with the writings of most of the Fugitives. One could scarcely expect that the literary renown in which the leading members of the group were held at the time of the 1956 Reunion would still be theirs in the last decade of the twentieth century. Even so, their best work is still very much alive, and no history of modern American letters can overlook them and the day of their flourishing.

I knew them all. What an amazing group of men they were! They had their faults, their vanities, their blind spots, as who has not. I was not back in the South for very long before I came to see what was so wrong about Davidson's stand on civil rights; and Tate's conservative politics were not for me. Hindsight is perceptive in that respect. No matter. That I was actually present at that 1956 Reunion and privileged to watch these men in action together seems ever more astounding. I stand by a line of verse from the poet they had come most to admire, Yeats: "All the Olympians; a thing never known again."

(1994)

Cleanth Brooks (1907–1994):
A Memory

He liked good talk. Conversation was a joy to him. He had a wide range of interests, read the newspapers, watched television, kept up with what was going on. There was always something to talk about.

In the years after his wife's death in 1986 he usually came down once or twice a year for visits of several days at a time. We have a mostly Siamese cat, which whenever Cleanth arrived seemed to think it owned him. No sooner did Cleanth enter the house and take a seat in the living room than the cat positioned itself alongside his chair and proceeded to attack his hands; they played back and forth, with Cleanth talking to us all the while, until we decided the cat had received enough attention from him and chased it away. Cleanth liked the cat, too; "he does very well for a little predator," he would remark while tussling with it. He would discourse at length on cats and dogs and predators, and the pack instinct. Our cat probably wonders why he didn't come down this past spring.

In the summer of 1992 we made a trip to Scotland, Cleanth, my wife and myself, with the ambition of following Johnson's and Boswell's route through the Hebrides in 1773. We took a late evening Northwest Air Lines plane from Boston. Cleanth, who was slight of physical stature, curled up in his seat and slept for much of the six-hour flight. My wife and I are both on the hefty side, and the seats aboard the DC–10 jet were cruelly narrow; we got no sleep at all.

Arrangements at the airport at Glasgow were terribly disorganized; one would have thought it was Palermo or Casablanca. The morning was almost over before we were aboard a train for Edinburgh. By then my wife and I had been awake for something like twenty-two hours. While Cleanth talked about Scottish place-names, it was all we could do to keep our eyes open.

With a former student of mine from years ago who lives in the Highlands doing the driving, we spent a dozen fine days in pursuit of Boswell and Johnson. We couldn't go everywhere that the eighteenth-century travelers went, but we came fairly close. Cleanth was eighty-five at the time, but each morning he was first down to breakfast, and he outwalked us throughout the Hebrides. I had brought along a copy of Boswell's account, and between that and the *Blue Guide* we had a quite decent introduction to the country we traversed, while Cleanth's commentary on British history and related topics was ongoing and sparkling. I think of it now as a lost opportunity. If only I'd brought along a cassette recorder or taken notes I might have produced a travel book of my own, entitled *A Journey Through the Western Isles of Scotland with Cleanth Brooks, B.A., B. Litt. (Oxon.), Litt.D.*

There was another occasion in particular when I also wish I'd had a tape recorder deployed. It was back in 1952 or 1953. Cleanth had come to lecture at the Johns Hopkins University, where I was an instructor in what is now called the Writing Seminars. After his talk, at a party at our apartment, Cleanth and the great Romance philological scholar Leo Spitzer, and the French phenomenological critic Georges Poulet happily engaged in a two-hour discussion about the way to read a poem, while the rest of us listened. It was a show indeed—Spitzer, with his deep-voiced German-inflected asseverations, and Cleanth's gentle but indefatigable accents of sweet reasonableness. Poulet, by temperament no monologist, was outgunned conversationally; he did his best to get his oar in—"but isn't there also a sense in which there's an ideal poem that the poet wishes to write, but . . . " But he was up against a pair of major league argufyers. Spitzer was in his glory; *"L'esprit de l'escalier!"* he declared happily as the evening ended and all were departing.

Cleanth had enormous patience, great kindness, and, when it came to literary matters, a missionary zeal. He was ever ready to talk with students and others when asked. Late one evening at a South Atlantic Modern Language Association convention in Atlanta, after a full day of activities followed by a dinner party at a restaurant somewhere out in the suburbs, a group of us straggled back into the hotel close to midnight. It had been an evening with liquid refreshment, and by then I and others were ready to collapse from exhaustion. "Well," Cleanth remarked, "I'd better be turning in. I've got a breakfast appointment at seven o'clock with a young woman who's writing her dissertation on Faulkner." Seven o'clock! Nine would have been too early for me.

On another occasion, also at a S.A.M.L.A. meeting in Atlanta, Cleanth and I were seated in front of the Louisiana State University Press booth talking late one afternoon, and a young man, obviously a graduate student somewhere, came up and interrupted our conversation. "I'd like to ask you a question," he announced without warning. "What is the place of Erskine Caldwell in southern literature?"

Just about the last thing in the world that I felt like doing at that moment was entering into a discussion with anyone, right out of the blue so to speak, on the subject of Erskine Caldwell, for whose work my admiration is decidedly limited. I shook my head and said something to the effect that it was too late in the day to talk about Caldwell. Not so Cleanth; he proceeded patiently to give the young man his thoughts on that writer. In other words, I might be too important to be bothered with talking to an eager young graduate student, but Cleanth Brooks was not. I felt rather ashamed—though not enough so to get involved in the conversation.

Both as literary critic and conversationalist, Cleanth took delight in developing metaphors. The first time I observed his penchant for figures of speech was at the Fugitives' Reunion in Nashville in 1956. Vanderbilt University had finally deigned to pay honor to that group of illustrious poets, and all were there—John Crowe Ransom, Allen Tate, Robert Penn Warren, Donald Davidson, Andrew Lytle, Merrill Moore, along with others such as William Yandell Elliott who following graduation had not continued to meditate the thankless muse with appropriate strictness. Although a year or so too young to have been a Fugitive himself, Cleanth soon afterward became a major force in helping them wage the pedagogical wars attending the upholding of the poetry of modernism, and as a literary figure he was certainly as prominent as any of the group.

The last of the Reunion's closed sessions centered on the Fugitives' early days, and Cleanth was asked to begin with some remarks on what, in the Vanderbilt and Nashville environment, had helped to produce or encourage the coming into being of so remarkable a group.

He opened by citing Samuel Johnson's remark about the poets of Pembroke College, Oxford: "Sir, we are a nest of singing birds." Johnson's phrase, he said, aptly characterized the present occasion. "We have been looking at a last year's bird nest—a rather glorious bird nest," he declared, to everyone's amusement. It was, indeed, a "bird's nest of considerably more splendor than the rather modest little nest" that Johnson had rejoiced in.

He was now off and running. Why, he asked, does one examine a bird's nest, "particularly when a good many of the birds have flown?" Even those birds "that remain in this habitat are no longer fledglings," and he noted Donald Davidson, "who spreads his own wings and beats the air powerfully." Many of the Fugitives have proved to be "migratory birds," living far away from Nashville. The study of bird-nest building, he said, might be considered an art— the study of the kind of community out of which literature grows. Dr. Johnson, he noted, called it "the art of nidification, bird-nest building."

At that point he dropped the figure, but soon returned to it. What is the use, he asked, of "the study of literary bird-nest building? Does anyone have the foolishness to think that thereby he can learn to build such a nest?" After comparing the situation as it had been at Vanderbilt in the 1920s with what he found at Yale University at the present time, he came back to his metaphor for one more turn. "Inspection of last year's bird's nest will not tell us how to make Vanderbilt once again a nest of singing birds," he declared. But—and, remaining in the garden, he shifted neatly from birds to their preferred diet—"Granted the need for talent, granted a great many other things, unless you have the proper seed bed, the proper nurturing circumstances, the seed of a literary movement perishes."

It was a vintage performance, and among other things exemplified why, as critic, Cleanth Brooks had been so drawn to the English Metaphysical poets.

His career might be said to have divided itself into two principal sectors. From the early 1930s until the early 1950s, he was concerned mainly, though never exclusively, with the reading and criticism of poetry—which is to say, with the New Criticism. It was during this period that he and Robert Penn Warren developed the textbook that served as principal lever in the pedagogical revolution that moved the study of poetry away from an emphasis upon source hunting and the history of ideas into the consideration of poems as unique literary artifacts. *Understanding Poetry* appeared first in 1938. It was followed a year later by Brooks's monograph, *Modern Poetry and the Tradition*. In 1947 came his *The Well Wrought Urn: Studies in the Structure of Poetry*. Those three books contain the Cleanth Brooks who, as literary critic, matters most of all.

In the late 1940s Cleanth's interest began turning toward the fiction of William Faulkner, and with the appearance of *William Faulkner: The Yoknapatawpha Country* in 1963, he became by all odds the foremost interpreter of our foremost twentieth-century novelist. Thirty years later, Cleanth's remains the critical assessment with which anyone who wishes to write on the subject must deal; there is no getting round it. He followed it up with three more books on Faulkner's work, but *The Yoknapatawpha Country* is the one that counts.

The last book he published during his lifetime, *Historical Evidence and the Reading of Seventeenth-Century Poetry* (1991), was a return to the reading of English poetry, this time to consider a group of poems by minor poets which required a knowledge of the history and the culture for their proper understanding. The book constituted an effort—surely an unnecessary one—to demonstrate the falsity of the charges commonly leveled at him as a New Critic. He was alleged to have contended in *The Well Wrought Urn* and other books that extrinsic information such as history and biography was without importance in reading poems, and that therefore the dominant graduate-school training in literature was useless. "I trust," he wrote, "that the preceding chapters constitute solid testimony to my own regard for the importance of establishing authorship, datings, biographical and historical references, and the specific and sometimes archaic uses of words that make up the poet's text."

Anyone who, having read *The Well Wrought Urn*, was myopic enough to think Brooks believed history unimportant, was unlikely to be convinced otherwise by another book. I suspect the truth was that Cleanth had had his say on Faulkner, and since he dearly loved reading and explicating Jacobean and Caroline poems, the refutation of accusations of his supposed ahistoricity offered as good an excuse as any for yet another engagement with the verse of the period.

He also went back, however lightly, to the subject of his first book, *The Relation of the Alabama-Georgia Dialect to the Provincial Dialects of Great Britain* (1935), and produced another little volume on southern speech, *The Language of the American South* (1985), developing his point that rural southern upcountry dialect was not a corruption of the English language, but a survival of what had been the normal speech of certain southern English counties prior to the eighteenth century. Thus, what was thought to be black southern mispronunciation of standard English, as for example "dat" for "that," was no such thing, but was instead the retention of inflections the slaves had picked up when they first learned to speak English during the colonial period. The book embroiled him in more controversy, for it was interpreted by some of the militant black scholars as a sneaky attempt to minimize the African heritage by claiming that what were thought of as distinctively black speech patterns were originally borrowings from white speech. Cleanth was startled, for no such consideration had remotely crossed his mind, but by then he was accustomed to being a prime object of academic attack, most of it irrational, and he did not let it perturb him unduly.

Robert B. Heilman has remarked on the seeming anomaly of this mild-mannered, agreeable little man's having become the target of so much vituperation from structuralists, deconstructionists, feminists, practitioners of the so-called New Literary History, black militants, and whatever. "To charge Brooks with error," Heilman wrote, "has become one way of symbolizing one's professional reliability, independence, and deserts." There was a time when scarcely an issue of *Critical Inquiry* appeared without one or more persons pronouncing anathema on Cleanth. There and elsewhere he was pronounced an elitist, reactionary, escapist, obscurantist, obfuscator, covert Christian, sexist, neo-Confederate, fascist, imperialist, racist, Cold War warrior, defender of the *status quo ante Marston Moor,* etc., etc. The assault has not so much slackened as simply become old hat.

Why Brooks, one might wonder, but not Warren? After all, *Understanding Poetry* was very much a collaborative effort, as were *Understanding Fiction* (1943), *An Approach to Literature* (1936), and *Modern Rhetoric* (1949). Yet it is Cleanth, not Red Warren, who is customarily singled out for hostile attention. He has even been censured for supposedly having lured Red away from his true account as poet and novelist into the writing and editing of textbooks, which is utter nonsense, for in fact it was Red, until the late 1940s always much in need of extra income, who was repeatedly the instigator of such revenue-producing projects.

Part of the answer is that the fashion of Cleanth-bashing was given effective and early impetus by some of his impatient younger colleagues in the Yale English Department, who came to make up the so-called Yale School of Deconstructionism, since largely scattered ("Yale School, my ass!" to quote Warren on the subject.) Unlike Warren, Brooks was very much a full-time working member of the English department. He directed dissertations, played an active role in all academic deliberations, and thus exemplified the approach to literary study of his generation of scholars as well as the Repressive Establishment that stood in the way of their being able to run the show. Moreover, Warren was not only a critic and pedagogue but also a widely published poet and novelist; and theories of *écriture* notwithstanding, academic critics tend to be leery of attacking actual practitioners of literature while they are still alive and able to retaliate. Cleanth, on the other hand, being neither poet nor novelist but only a critic writing about other people's poems and novels, was fair game.

Another reason for Cleanth's attractiveness as a target was the persistence with which he went about arguing his case as a critic. He made his point, reinforced it, approached it via another route and made it again, and returned to it recurrently to keep it fresh in the reader's mind. Seldom did he raise his voice; almost never did he bandy insults. But he stayed on the trail with the doggedness of a working bloodhound and would not be diverted. Holding strong views, he was not afraid to express them. Moreover, he was not above proceeding to his objective via a roundabout route, in order to anticipate and neutralize the expected objections.

He was a master of what, in military tactics, is known as the refused flank—the deliberate withdrawal out of normal alignment in order to contain the enemy's assault and set the scene for a counterattack. Thus the opening paragraph of the chapter on Wordsworth's "Ode: Intimations of Immortality from Recollections of Early Childhood" in *The Well Wrought Urn:*

> Wordsworth's great "Intimations" ode has been for so long intimately connected with Wordsworth's own autobiography, and indeed, Wordsworth's poems in general have been so consistently interpreted as documents pertaining to that autobiography, that to consider one of his larger poems as an object in itself may actually seem impertinent. Yet to do so for once at least is not to condemn the usual mode of procedure and it may, in fact, have positive advantages.

Far be it from him to wish to upset any academic applecarts. Irony and paradox in Wordsworth? Heavens, no! Saints Garrod, Harper, and Raymond D. Havens preserve us! (Brutus is an honorable man.) All that he has in mind is just this one little illustrative job of close reading, following which the professorate can resume with business as usual.

He intends, of course, no such thing, and the academic Old Guard knows that, too. What he is really saying is: Look, the Immortality Ode is a poem, and I am now going to read it as such, and if it can't stand up to the same close scrutiny as any other good poem, then that's just too bad. By putting the matter the way he does, he has issued a challenge that the Old Guard can't very well refuse to pick up. Moving with exasperating thoroughness he then proceeds to read Wordsworth's poem his way and finds that, although it is not without flaws, on the whole it works quite well.

The Well-Wrought Urn was published at just about the time—1947—when it was becoming difficult to deny tenure to an assistant professor merely for having evinced an undue interest in the texture vs. structure dispute, or for being caught with a copy of the *Kenyon Review* in a faculty mailbox. Some notable citadels were still conspicuously holding out, but in most places the moat had been bridged and the defensive works breached.

Not only that, but there was Cleanth Brooks, no longer a resident of Baton Rouge, Louisiana, now living and working in New Haven, Connecticut! A New Critic, a diehard southerner and Agrarian sympathizer, had become a professor at Yale, that epicenter of eighteenth-century historico-biographical scholarship. It was as if Jonathan Edwards had been made a prelate and given an office suite at the Vatican. ("Cleanth says he's boring from within, but I think they're boring from within Cleanth," said Allen Tate, who had a wicked tongue.)

There was a brief period, in the 1950s, when the New Criticism was indeed almost a kind of orthodoxy. In Robert Heilman's words, "Some enthusiastic converts seized new terminologies and brandished them so relentlessly that useful instruments seemed hackneyed. For years it was as if some seductive ad had proclaimed, 'Symbols can be fun' or 'Make every day your symbol day.' " Yet if the New Criticism did for a time become the predominant approach to literature in college and university English departments (I think Heilman's "for years" exaggerates the duration of its ascendancy), assuredly it could scarcely have been because of the supposed ideological and political implications that have been read into its practice in recent years—i.e., covert Anglican homiletics, defense of the status quo, conservative bias, card-carrying elitism, etc.

To be sure, in the years just after World War II there was something of a High Church vogue in English departments, with T. S. Eliot as resident apostle. Christian Existentialism was in style; I think it was Auden who wrote of "a time of significant conversions." But for the most part it was deeply personal stuff, and can scarcely account for the thoroughness with which the New Criticism registered upon readers of poetry. In the same way, the claim that insistence upon the integrity of the poem as a self-contained aesthetic artifact was a subterfuge for dodging the relevance of social issues will not hold water. One might as plausibly assert that the consideration of Goya's *Los Desastres de la Guerra* or Picasso's *Guernica* in terms of their artistic dimensions is a way of avoiding what they had to say about the making of war, or that any attempt by a musicologist to approach Beethoven's *Symphony No. 3 in E-Flat Major* through melodic development and chordal progression, rather than the composer's decision to remove the original dedication after Napoleon proclaimed himself emperor, constitutes an effort to evade its political implications.

The notion that the exploration of a literary work's complexity serves as a discouragement to its usefulness as an impetus to social action, and therefore is a covert way of enforcing the status quo, is highly dubious reasoning. The same objection could be made about *any* approach to literature other than as straight ideological activism. If an encouragement to social action is what is desired, there are far more efficient ways to achieve that than by discussing poems. The statement really amounts to no more than the assertion that during the reading of a poem someone is not also likely to be engaged in casting a vote, building a garage, or sighting a rifle. Likewise, to the kindred accusation that the New Criticism, by demanding that the components of a poem work with and against each other as part of a totality, places a premium upon order and thus inhibits all change and social amelioration, one can only respond that precisely the same objection could be made to a manufacturer of intercontinental ballistic missiles or a designer of golf courses.

As for the New Criticism being "elitist," why of course it is. So also is the study of any of the fine arts. So is governmental subsidy of noncommercial public television and FM radio broadcasting stations "elitist"; how many members of the working class watch Masterpiece Theater or listen to classical music? Is there any way of applying one's intelligence and imagination to the reading of poems by John Keats, rather than to the reading of poems by Bob Dylan, that is not "elitist"? But that either the New Criticism's "elitism" in general, or Cleanth's in particular, involved anything resembling snobbery, exclusiveness, economic victimization of the underprivileged, or racial, religious, or sexual discrimination, I deny emphatically. There have been few better small-d democrats than Cleanth Brooks.

Such arguments miss the point. They are insufficient to account for the swiftness with which the New Criticism swept through the educational cosmos and permanently altered the way that poetry was being taught. Surely it wasn't its alleged theoretical implications about the nature of God, man, and society that gave the New Criticism its impetus. Its appeal lay in its *method,* not in any implied theory of literature or society. It was not another scheme for *interpreting* poems, relating them to life, to human experience, and so on. Rather, it was a way of *reading* them in order to facilitate interpretation. It was, and it remains, just about the only way yet developed for reading poems that can potentially open them up to full appreciation by the reader. Nor, despite claims to the contrary, does its application rule out, or for that matter even hinder, any and all other approaches, whether ideological or textual.

All it does—and it is a very great deal—is to ask that a poem be looked at intrinsically, word by word, image by image, line by line, and stanza by stanza, in terms of what is present on the printed page, and that the various constituent parts be read in concert as they exist and function within the poem. Nowadays we mostly take that for granted. In Heilman's words, the revolution that Brooks and Warren and their allies worked "is likely to be permanent; unless we are unlucky we will not lose our knowledge that literature exists in its own right, not as a subheading of social history, and that its structures define its essence." This is true, I think, of all but the most extreme ideologically based criticisms of our own day.

If so, then why the hostility? Once again, why is Cleanth, as the New Criticism's leading workman, so often anathematized?

What it comes down to, I think, is that no small portion of the resentment he seemed to incur was the result of sheer exasperation.

That is to say, to be able to do what he did so well required, and requires, among other things, a willingness to stay with poetry *as* poetry, to take continuing pleasure in the specifically literary properties of poems. To read a poem attentively and well demands patience, alertness, and intelligence. It also requires imagination, the kind that can be alive to nuances and relationships, and that can pick up the connotative as well as the denotative properties of words. It follows that anyone who cannot actively enjoy that kind of reading, for its own sake, on a sustained basis, but aches to go racing ahead and link the poem up to this or that extrinsic concern before exploring its details, is apt to lose patience with Cleanth and his way of doing things.

In arguing for the importance of irony and paradox within poems, the New Critics came up against a paradox themselves, one that had been roiling the waters at least since the time of Plato and Aristotle. This was, that (a) unless a literary work is about life, it is of no interest to anyone; but (b) it is *not* life, and its success and readability depend upon how well the raw life is transmuted into art—i.e., shaped into literary form. If, therefore, the work of literature, being about life, is by definition at one remove from life itself, then those who teach literature and who write about it are at *two* removes from it. What this meant (and still very much means) is that teachers of literature tend to feel themselves cut off from the real world, and barred, to the extent they are professionals, from having any direct dealings with real life.

Once the excitement of the triumph over the Old Guard died down, therefore, and the novelty of being enabled to read poems as self-sustaining literary artifacts wore off, the old discomfort at being at two removes from real life asserted itself. It was not long, therefore, before the profession began once again to seize upon the various emerging opportunities for supposedly placing literary study in the direct service of real life. I shan't take up each development individually; suffice it to say that they have followed along, one after the other, and the end is by no means in sight.

Yet all the while, there was Cleanth Brooks, with his devotion to tracing out the complexity of poems. Yes, but have you thought about this image, and considered how it undercuts that one? If the poem says what you say it does, then why is that stanza included? How can you reconcile what seems to be happening here with what you claim is the overall thrust of the poem? Why couldn't the man see that there were more important things going on in this world than poems? Preach! Write! Act! Do anything, save to sit down and read Eliot and Donne!

I exaggerate; it was not so simple as that. But it does seem difficult to account for the insult that rained down on Cleanth Brooks from so many quarters merely for the ideological reasons customarily cited. Others have exhibited these alleged shortcomings without attracting the kind of barrage directed at Cleanth. The variety and the ferocity of the anti-Brooks onslaught lead one to suspect that something else might be at issue, and that the grievances customarily cited might well be not so much the source of the outcry as the rationalization of an underlying plaint.

I have the sense that as critic of poetry Cleanth symbolized, or embodied, something that both irritated and threatened many academics, and that this had less to do with his views than to the fact of his presence on the scene—a careful reader of poems, content to do so, feeling no compulsion to demonstrate either to others or to himself that he was something more immediately useful or relevant, but also alert to show up misreadings, whether made through laziness or pedantic turn of mind or both. In sticking to his trade as explicator of poems, Cleanth exemplified what a *literary* scholar should be, and for that very reason he incurred resentment, of much the same sort as the response of that Athenian citizen who voted to send Aristides into exile because he was "tired of hearing him called 'The Just' all the time."

Cleanth was, in short, a kind of academic father figure. White, male, Protestant, calm, reasonable, interested in poetry as poetry, he was a walking rebuke to ideologues and would-be activists of all shapes and varieties. His very presence was a threat. "Avaunt! and quit my sight! let the earth hide thee!" *Ecrasez l'infâme!*

The majority of the more virulent attacks on Cleanth have been based on his role as New Critic of poetry. His writings on William Faulkner also have occasioned criticism, mainly to the effect that— again, in conservative defense of the status quo—he has attempted to tame the violence in that novelist's fiction in order to make him into a conservator of traditional values instead of the savage rebel against complacency and injustice that the creator of Thomas Sutpen, Joe Christmas, and Jason Compson so unabashedly was.

Now I believe that there *is* an argument that can be made against the way that Cleanth has handled Faulkner's fiction. But it does not have much to do with any supposed conservative defense of the status quo. What Cleanth did tend to do, I think, was to overreact to any criticism of the South by outsiders. It was *not* that he sought to justify or to explain away the existence of evil and injustice in the South, whether Old or New, but rather that he sometimes made a fetish of insisting that things were equally as bad or worse elsewhere. He could not sit idly by and see Faulkner's complex storytelling genius oversimplified and distorted into little morality plays.

I think it no coincidence that it was after the move to New England that his principal interest as a critic shifted from poetry to the fiction of William Faulkner. It is an oft-observed phenomenon that an awareness of southern identity tends to intensify once one leaves the South. That Cleanth, as a student of literature and not long after joining the English faculty at Yale, should have begun to take a special interest in the novels of the South's foremost teller of tales is understandable. The fecundity of Faulkner's literary imagination and the complexity of much of his writings, in style and shape and in the author's attitude toward the community and its formidable burden of history and myth, offered an intriguing prospect to someone only recently removed from that community himself and very much aware of its hold on his own imagination. In a very real sense, to explore Faulkner's fiction was to explore Cleanth's consciousness.

When *William Faulkner: The Yoknapatawpha Country* appeared in 1963, a number of books had been published on Faulkner, including at least one quite good study by Olga Vickery. Cleanth's book, however, constituted a far more imaginative and richer reading of the fiction, undertaken in terms of Faulkner's abiding involvement in the land and the people who inhabit it. His training as a careful reader of poems served him well, in that before coming to conclusions about what was going on in a story, he made sure he had accounted for all the evidence.

The most striking example of this is in his handling of the events of *Absalom, Absalom!* A great deal of that story's significance depends upon discovering what really happened, as distinct from what might have been generally believed to have happened at the time. In other words, a kind of detective story, in which the truth not only lies concealed, but indeed can never be fully determined but only conjectured. So what Cleanth proceeded to do was to work up a chart in which he listed the ultimate authority for various facts and events, determined who did or didn't know various important facts, and which conjectures about facts and events were made by which characters.

The result is, to say the least, startling. It becomes evident that a great many of the supposed facts in the story are not facts at all, but only assumptions. Important actions take place on the basis of conjectures made by the characters in the novel. Information seemingly with crucial bearing upon the outcome is shown to be no more than hypothetical. Moreover, the fact that the characters and the narrator do not know whether some important assumptions are true or not, so that as readers *we* can't know, either, is no mere narrative device. It is a central aspect of the novel's meaning. Needless to say, Cleanth's careful reading of Faulkner's novel had the result of undercutting not a few previously published interpretations of *Absalom, Absalom!*

I have no wish to get into the particulars of either the disputes or the interpretation. But I have to say that at least part of Cleanth's motivation for writing about *Absalom, Absalom!* clearly had to do with the wish to knock the props from under certain sweeping sociological generalizations about the Old South made by several commentators, and I do think that both the remarkable strengths and also the liabilities of his critical engagement with Faulkner's fiction can be identified in his handling of *Absalom, Absalom!*

Much of his attention is focussed upon the figure of Thomas Sutpen, the ruthless, driving, awesomely ambitious poor white whose effort not only to carve a plantation out of the antebellum Mississippi wilderness but to establish a dynasty that will endure beyond his own mortality constitutes the action upon which everything else that happens in the story ultimately depends. What makes Sutpen's plantation possible, and also brings about his downfall, is slavery, and the attitude toward race that allowed the South's "peculiar institution" to flourish in its time and place.

Cleanth takes considerable pains to demonstrate that Sutpen is *not* a typical or representative antebellum planter, and he insists that, both in what Sutpen does and the way he goes about doing it, he is "on all fours with the robber baron of the Gilded Age building a fake Renaissance palace on the banks of the Hudson." He stresses the abstraction in Sutpen's "design," and declares that he would "seize upon 'the traditional' as a pure abstraction—which, of course, is to deny its very meaning." The tradition, he says, "is an assortment of things to be possessed, not a manner of living that embodies certain values and determines man's conduct. The fetish objects are to be gained by sheer ruthless efficiency." In other words, *Absalom, Absalom!* constitutes no easy parable of the sins of the Old South, and Thomas Sutpen's wicked deeds are committed not merely because he is a southern slaveholder but because he is a flawed human being.

All of which is quite true. Yet the fact remains that *Absalom, Absalom!*, though in its implications it may not be exclusively about the Old South, is nonetheless deeply grounded in the particularities of southern history and southern experience. It is *not* about robber barons building Renaissance palaces along the Hudson River, but about its author's own Mississippi heritage. Whether Thomas Sutpen is a "typical" or "representative" antebellum slaveholder isn't the issue; it was the existence of the "Peculiar Institution" in the Old South that made possible the particular career chronicled in the novel.

The point is that the agonizing struggle of young Quentin Compson to come to terms with the history and the racial attitudes of his community lay at the very heart of the experience not only of William Faulkner but of twentieth-century southern writing in general— including a certain critical work by a southern author named Cleanth Brooks. For clearly it was Cleanth's resistance to the indictment of the South from the outside that led him again and again to stress the relevance of Faulkner's story to other regions of the country as well, and to write paragraphs such as the following:

> Sutpen belongs to the company of Conrad's Kurtz (though perhaps Kurtz did learn something at the very end; Marlow thinks that he did.) But it is not difficult to find his compeers closer to home. I have already suggested that we might search for them with good hope of success among the brownstone mansions of post–Civil War New York. But it is easy to locate them in recent fiction. As was remarked in an earlier chapter, the Southern novelists of our time have been fascinated by this kind of character, perhaps because for them he still has some aura of the monstrous, and is still not quite to be taken for granted.

The implication is that, since in ambition and ruthlessness Thomas Sutpen is like a European such as Marlow's Kurtz or like a post-1865 New York financial mogul, the South can't very well be singled out for special blame. More than that, the frequent presence of such characters in modern southern fiction comes about not because they are any more prevalent in southern experience than elsewhere, but because southern novelists continue to consider them monstrous. Presumably, novelists born and reared elsewhere find them and their conduct in no way unusual or atypical.

Needless to say, this is not literary analysis so much as sectional defense, whereby the critic labors to counteract the propensity of William Faulkner to provide fiction that inadvertently gives aid and comfort to what for Cleanth is still, to an extent at least, the enemy: to wit, northern-based critics, otherwise known as Yankees.

What I would insist is that if at various places throughout his study of Faulkner, Cleanth is at great pains to keep the various novels from being read as indictments of the South as such, and expends so much ingenuity seeking to anticipate and invalidate possible censure of his and Faulkner's native region, this ardent involvement is likewise the source of much of the book's strength. For what makes *William Faulkner: The Yoknapatawpha Country* the acutely insightful work of literary criticism that it is was in no small part the result of the creative tension engendered by the debate between its author's critical rigor, on the one hand, and his emotional involvement with the South, on the other. Surely what impelled Cleanth to try to get to the bottom of what really happens in *Absalom, Absalom!* was at least in part a response to holier-than-thou critical interpretations which depicted the book as a simple allegory of the wickedness of the antebellum South. Had it not meant so much, emotionally as well as intellectually, to him, Cleanth would never have felt the compulsion to dig so deeply, and, in so doing, to discover so much that is important to the full understanding of the story.

His major book on Faulkner is a labor of love, a flawed critical masterpiece, which I daresay might never have been written had Cleanth not left L.S.U. for Yale University in 1947 and found there, in his graduate and undergraduate classes, numerous intelligent and imaginative students whose view of everyday life in the American South was a compound of *Gone With the Wind, Tobacco Road,* and the Scottsboro Seven. "You cant understand it," Quentin Compson tells his Canadian roommate Shreve McCannon in *Absalom, Absalom!* "You would have to be born there." Cleanth made it possible for them to understand it, or more properly, made it possible for William Faulkner to help them understand it.

He had an affinity for Faulkner. I like to think of him and his passion for explication and good talk in terms of the Nobel Prize Address: " . . . when the last ding-dong of doom has clanged and faded from the last worthless rock hanging tideless in the last red and dying evening, there will still be one more sound: that of his puny inexhaustible voice, still talking."

Ann Waldron, in *Hodding Carter: The Reconstruction of a Racist* (1993), tells of an incident whereby the future Pulitzer Prize–winning newspaper editor and Cleanth, who roomed together as graduate students at Tulane University in 1928, went up to Baton Rouge to be interviewed for Rhodes Scholarships. Both were engaged to be married, Cleanth to Tinkum Blanchard and Carter to Betty Werlein. At the last moment Carter decided not to go into the building and take the examination. "I don't think Betty will wait for me while I am in England," he said. (Rhodes Scholars were required to remain unmarried during their three-year stays at Oxford.)

"Tinkum will wait for me," Cleanth declared. So, while Hodding Carter sat outside in the automobile and wrote a poem, he went into the building, passed the exam, and won the scholarship.

They were married in 1934, and to say that it was a good marriage would be a considerable understatement. When Tinkum died, Cleanth's friends feared for his welfare, for if ever there was a man well looked after by a wife, it was Cleanth. Tinkum—her given name was Edith May, which she much disliked—not only took care of the house and property, did the cooking and cleaning, saw that he was properly attired, and so on, but also handled all the family finances, did all the highway driving, and typed his manuscripts.

To the surprise and delight of their friends, however, Cleanth bravely squared up to the requirements of a cruelly diminished situation. He learned to do for himself the many things that Tinkum had taken care of, to handle the finances, get his manuscripts typed, make travel arrangements, and otherwise resume a very active professional and social life. Indeed, observing him in his travels and watching him take such delight in talking with friends, one might not at first have realized how bereft he was throughout the seven years following Tinkum's death and before his own. Several years later he confided in my wife how greatly he continued to miss Tinkum. As well he might.

In any event, he *did* come back. Indeed, when we were touring the Hebrides with him in 1992 he even went so far as to remark, to our considerable alarm, that he had in mind to get his automobile driver's license reinstated, and to resume driving his car! Fortunately, given the weakness of his peripheral vision through those quarter-inch-thick eyeglass lenses, he did not carry through with this particular resolve.

He was active almost until the very end. In February of 1994 he traveled to England to lecture at the University of London. The trip, he reported, was more tiring than usual. He wrote that he found "that although with a little alcohol and some lively talk, I could liven up and do a lot of talking myself—probably too much talking—I also, once I was alone by myself, got terribly quiet and tired and had to do a lot of napping and sleeping." After a week in London he met an old friend with whom he had played Rugby football at Exeter College in Oxford in 1929–1932, and "we had two or three very pleasant days in Oxford revisiting our old college and being allowed to dine at the high table."

He returned home to prepare to start radiology treatments for "my little tumor." His doctors, he wrote, told him that they didn't expect to cure him, but did hope "to keep me happy and comfortable for the next while. I inquired naturally how long that while might be expected to be and they told me frankly that they didn't know. They did say that people in my fix sometimes lived six months and some five years and that I seemed pretty healthy in general but we shall see, we shall see."

He wasn't feeling particularly depressed, he said; "I'm eighty-seven and had hardly expected to get to ninety, surely not above ninety, so I'm not unduly worried about the state of affairs, but I do have a lot of things to clear up and clean up before I say farewell." In any event he hoped to "pay a little visit to Chapel Hill in the months to come and have a real visit . . . "

The letter was dated March 16. He did not make it. Once the radiology treatments began he lost ground rapidly. On May 12, 1994, he died.

Not too long before his death, he was asked to read the manuscript of a book about himself. He hadn't, he said, even known it was in the works. "I have read a good deal of it and I must say it is a friendly reviewer who writes well and I hope for the best with it but it's a very queer state of mind to find yourself in, when a book is being written about you and you find yourself wondering did I really do this, did I really say that. Why didn't he put it just this way rather than that way? Then you have to keep reminding yourself that this book is being written by somebody else, not by you . . . "

In years to come there will very likely be much written about him. One can only hope that the vogue for parricide will wear off, so that ambitious young academics will no longer feel it profitable to demonstrate their fealty to assorted critical causes by savaging the man who more than any other critic living or dead taught them how to read poems. When and if that day ever arrives, perhaps Cleanth will come in, if only posthumously, for more of the gratitude and veneration that should be his from those who follow his chosen profession. I like Lewis Simpson's way of putting it. He is describing the several books that Cleanth and Red Warren edited; they have, he says, "enhanced the literary quality of American life." We are all better readers because of Cleanth Brooks.

(1995)

In Memory of Howard Nemerov
(1920–1991)

Howard Nemerov has been dead for just under two months as I write this (in early September), and I see that I am going to keep right on missing him for as long as I live. It is a matter of knowing he was there—and that certain things that I thought were amusing would be thought amusing by him, too, and vice versa.

I was thinking yesterday about Harold Bloom and how pretentious and preposterous his whole critical operation is, and I got out Howard's *Figures of Thought* and read again his marvelously comic demolition of *The Anxiety of Influence.* He said it so well and clearly, and I wanted to call him and tell him so—and I couldn't. That is what missing someone means.

Usually he would call up long distance, out of the blue, and we would chat—though I hasten to say that he wasn't easy to chat casually with on the telephone. When he called it was really to say *How are you? I'm thinking of you. I miss you.* By calling he was saying that, and the conversation itself was pretty much perfunctory.

About three weeks before he died, he called me to say goodbye. I was embarrassed. I shouldn't have been: I should have known, after thirty years, that there was to be no pretending, no arm's-length decorum. I told him what was true, that a great deal of his poetry had been written about precisely what he was currently engaged in doing. He apparently hadn't thought of that, and asked for chapter-and-verse, so I sat down and sent him chapter-and-verse. Whether by the time that my letter arrived he was still able to read it, I don't know; his wife Peggy said he went out within a few days after his call and couldn't read. But it was true. He had figured out, a long time back, long before any illness, that because he was going to die, everything he or anyone could say or think or do was to that extent a compromised, crucially limited activity, that was of qualified significance—and that if he was going to write anything really meaningful about human experience he had to start with that assumption. So that was usually what his poems were about: beyond this point we cannot know anything. Such victories as were won against time, against meaninglessness, were therefore conditional. So when he received the word that the growth on his esophagus was about to cut off the needed flow of blood to his brain and he would have to die soon, it was not as if he hadn't thought about it until then.

Knowing he was dying, would soon go, I thought *Now he'll finally find out, but this time he won't be able to write a poem and tell us about it.* And neither could he write a poem about that either. He would finally be Silence. What a deprivation for those who, like me, always relied upon him to go one step further on, look around carefully, and report back on what he saw. There would be nobody to give me news about myself any more—at least not with the perception and unblinking honesty that he could do it.

We met at Bread Loaf in 1961; we were both on the faculty. I invited him to come to Hollins College, Virginia, as writer-in-residence for 1962–1963, and because he had pretty much had it with Bennington College by then, he accepted. Of our writers-in-residence he was by far the best teacher we ever had—a superb classroom teacher. We gave the advanced creative-writing class together; it met Wednesday evening in my basement. Three weeks out of four he would come in, listen to some poems, and then after a time begin a commentary so brilliant that the students and I would simply sit there and listen, jaws hanging open in wonder. What he could think of to say about poetry was incredible. The fourth week he would be in a black mood, and a pall would descend upon the occasion, so heavy that I would spend much of the evening trying to lift it. One evening he came in, disgruntled, and snarled something. I wasn't feeling compassionate, so I snarled right back. "I just want to find something to bite at that won't bite back," he said, "Well, go look somewhere else," I told him. That seemed to calm him down, and the remainder of the evening went well.

Years earlier I had started out as a morning newspaperman and had never thrown the late-hours schedule. I always read until early morning in my basement study, while listening to music on the phonograph; and often he would drop by unannounced, listen with me, and talk. Both of us were interested in dream theory and psychoanalysis—he knew a great deal more about it than I did—and we used to speculate on dreams. We also formed the habit of often driving downtown to a delicatessen in Roanoke for lunch on Saturday mornings. We were seated in the delicatessen eating lunch once, and a salesman across the way began questioning us, blundering into, among other things, religion and the fact that we were Jewish. It was annoying, and Howard knew exactly how to handle him. "We're eating lunch and having a private conversation," he told the fellow, "and we'd like to be left alone." "Oh, I'm sorry," the salesman said, clearly discomfited. That was that. The salesman *had* been intrusive, not out of malice but because it was his egotistical way of conducting himself; he meant no harm. I wouldn't have had the nerve to say anything. Howard simply would not put up with any such unwarranted intrusion.

He taught one literature class, meeting it once a week. His office was across the hall from mine. He had been teaching for at least fifteen years, but he would come into my office a half-hour or so before the class was due to begin, puffing anxiously on a cigarette, highly nervous and agitated. For him each meeting was a public appearance, a performance. In his lifetime, in addition to his teaching, he must have made at least a thousand public appearances, reading poems or lecturing. Yet each was an ordeal, which he underwent because his career required it, or because his self-esteem demanded that he read his poems. He did it in a masterly way, but I had little sense that he enjoyed the actual doing itself. Late in his life, when he was poet laureate and finally had received the acclaim his poetry merited, this may have changed.

The year after he was at Hollins, when he was in Washington as consultant in poetry at the Library of Congress. I realized that he was going through a crisis. He was in a writing slump. Out of it came a book, *Journal of the Fictive Life*, published by the Rutgers University Press (1965), that did not win many laurels or attention, yet I thought it one of the most remarkable works of self-scrutiny and introspection ever written. One paragraph strikes me as appropriate just now: "The only way out is the way through, just as you cannot escape death except by dying. Being unable to write, you must examine in writing this being unable, which becomes for the present—henceforth?—the subject to which you are condemned."

Howard was difficult to be around; I have to say that. His letters were open and direct, but in person there was usually a barrier. He had little or no small talk. Except sometimes during the year at Hollins, when we saw each other all the time, I always felt a constraint in his company. We would meet again after several years, and spend a few hours together, or a day, or several days, but it was never relaxed. Was there anyone outside of his family with whom he could be completely at ease? I don't know, but I doubt it. I visited him in St. Louis several times, stayed with him and Peggy; we would listen to music, or he would play the piano for me, and talk some—but never without some awkwardness and periods of silence.

Howard did not have humor so much as wit. He was not the kind of person who laughed unrestrainedly. He liked to have me tell him jokes, which I heard from my brother in New York, but he did not burst into laughter at their ridiculousness or absurdity. The best he ever managed was a knowing smile. I remember him once telling me a Jewish joke, announcing that he was going to do so, and it wasn't funny. It was an idea, a paradox, not an absurdity or an incongruity. His mood was essentially melancholy, his wit mocking, often self-mocking.

He was always preoccupied, and typically with his career. He wanted recognition, very much, and toward the end, during the last ten or so years, he got it. He knew how very good a poet he was, and because he didn't play in the New York–Connecticut Literary Cocktail League he was a long time in having his unique excellence identified and credited. This irked him, as well it might.

Our backgrounds were very different. He grew up in a wealthy New York orthodox Jewish family. I grew up in a southern reform Jewish family. Both of us had long since shed our formal religious affiliations. We enjoyed each other's company as Jews, in part because neither of us defined ourselves in terms of our Jewishness. I thought of myself primarily as a southerner; he thought of himself primarily as a poet. My experience was middle class all the way; his was intellectual. He had been a spectacular undergraduate student at Harvard; in the American edition of *The Magic Mountain*, published in the late 1930s or early 1940s, Thomas Mann tells of having received a letter from an American undergraduate student named Howard Nemerov pointing out something about the novel that he had not himself recognized. This precocity was so foreign to my own experience, my own young manhood, that I could only marvel.

In effect we started from opposite ends of the spectrum and met in the middle; I had to learn about genuine artistic activity and achievement; Howard had to learn to be middle class and live in St. Louis. He was not a typical northeastern Ivy League or Manhattan-based intellectual; he did not thrive in intensely literary or advanced cultural company. He outgrew New York City and put the salon and the publisher's cocktail party behind him—though when necessary he attended them out of a sense of duty to his career. He learned to reject what I could never learn to accept. Coming at literature from opposite directions we arrived at the same place—a place that lay outside what was culturally fashionable and expedient.

But Howard was intelligent, brilliant, in a way that I was not and could never be. His capacity for abstract thought—or any other kind, for that matter—far exceeded mine. Not being from the South he did not have my interest in history, nor for his purposes did he need it. He had *wisdom*—insight into the human predicament. He saw and understood things. He once introduced me to an audience as "the sanest man I know"—which coming from a great poet was not entirely a compliment, though he intended it as such. I think what he meant was "practical" or "efficient" rather than "sane." Knowing mainly the academic and literary world, he might have thought that of me. (A businessman or politician would have known better.)

Whether he was a "major" or a "minor" poet I shall not dispute; what I am certain of is that at his best (which was often) he was a great poet. His poetry is unique in its magnificent fusion of idea and emotion in language. He was not afraid of thinking in his poems—yet neither was he cerebral. He wrote two kinds of poems. One kind was witty, acerbic, satirical; it was well done, but I did and do not care for it nearly as much as his lyric, philosophical, meditative poetry, so often about external nature—poems such as "The Blue Swallows," "Runes," "Summer's Elegy," "Two Girls," "Again." My favorite of all—though there are so many to choose from that I like—is his sestina, "Sarajevo," which inexplicably was omitted from the *Howard Nemerov Reader.* Perhaps I like it so much because it is historical, as few of his poems are. It is hauntingly beautiful; the complexity of the verse form is played against the matter and manner of saying.

The best of Nemerov is inimitable and wise and breathtakingly lovely. I'm going to say this: he was the best poet writing during his time, and ultimately this will be perceived, when the politics of our current poetry cease to operate and readers begin to look back and see what was written instead of who wrote it. In the important anthologies of the mid-twenty-first century (if there are any) there will be a half-dozen or more Nemerov poems.

In my memory he comes strolling across the Hollins campus from the post office, having collected the daily stack of mail (he worked hard at being a man of letters as well as writing his poems) wearing his heavy tan-gray leather jacket, whistling his odd tuneless whistle. He has something on his mind. *What is he thinking about today?*

(1991)

Acknowledgments

Nine of the pieces in this collection were first published in "Encaustics," the department that I conduct for the *Sewanee Review*. For permission to reprint them here, and for numerous other favors over the years, I am indebted to the editor of that distinguished magazine, George Core. The essays are:

"In Memory of Howard Nemerov," XCIX, 4 (Fall 1991):673–78.

"Literature and the Great War," C, 1 (Winter 1992):131–41.

"Babe Ruth's Ghost," CI, 2 (Spring 1993):240–47.

"Versions of the Kingfish," CI, 4 (Fall 1993):622–36.

"Sir William at the Hot Gates," CII, 1 (Winter 1994):176–80.

"The Grand Panjandrum of Wellfleet and Talcottville," CII, 3 (Summer 1994):496–506.

"Our Absolutely Deplorable Literary Situation—and Some Thoughts on How to Fix It Good," CII, 4 (Fall 1994):612–20.

"Cleanth Brooks: A Memory," CIII, 2 (Spring 1995):265–80.

"The Weasel's Twist, the Weasel's Tooth: The First World War as History," CIII, 3 (Summer 1995):429–39.

To Staige Blackford and the *Virginia Quarterly Review*, I am grateful for many acts of literary hospitality, including permission to reprint these essays:

"The Passionate Poet and the Use of Criticism," 68, 3 (Summer 1992):460–79.

"Did Churchill 'Ruin the Great Work of Time'? Thoughts on the New British Revisionism," 70, 1 (Winter 1994):59–78.

"H. L. Mencken of the Baltimore *Sunpapers*," 71, 2 (Spring 1995):189–209

The essay entitled "H. L. Mencken and the Baltimore *Sunpapers*" was originally delivered at the Enoch Pratt Free Library of Baltimore, Maryland, as part of its Mencken Day celebration, September 10, 1994.

I am indebted to Dave Smith and the *Southern Review* for permission to reprint the essay entitled "The Gathering of the Fugitives: A Recollection," 30, 4 (Autumn 1994):658–73.